DISCOVERY

DISCOVERY

Extraordinary results from everyday learning

John Drysdale

CYAN

Marshall Cavendish
Business

Copyright © 2005 John Drysdale

First published in Great Britain in 2005 by

Marshall Cavendish Business
An imprint of Marshall Cavendish International (Asia) Private Limited
A member of Times Publishing Limited
Times Centre, 1 New Industrial Road
Singapore 536196
T: +65 6213 9300
F: +65 6285 4871
E: *te@sg.marshallcavendish.com*
Online bookstore: *www.marshallcavendish.com/genref*

and

Cyan Communications Limited
4.3 The Ziggurat
60–66 Saffron Hill
London EC1N 8QX
www.cyanbooks.com

A CIP record for this book is available from the British Library

ISBN 981 261 803 1 (Asia & ANZ)

ISBN 1-904879-23-3 (Rest of world)

Designed and typeset by Curran Publishing Services, Norwich, UK

Printed and bound in Singapore

For Pru, Cameron, and Gavin

Use what talents you possess: the woods would be very silent if no birds sang there except those that sang best.

Henry Van Dyke

CONTENTS

ACKNOWLEDGMENTS

I would like to thank all these curious people whose insights have illuminated the discoveries we made together. Their generosity of spirit enabled me and I hope will help others to find learning in unexpected places.

Jacqueline Abbott Deane; Andy Armstrong; William Ayot; Alison Ball; Sally Bibb; Liam Black; Alan Boulton; Anne Bowerman; Paul Brown; Julian Burton; Michael Butler; Jane Clark; Isobel Davies; Rick Denton; Jim Dredge; Cathy Dunn; Fiona Gilvey; Kevin Graham; Markus Graw; David Hadfield; Robert Henderson; Robert Hiscox; Jeremy Kourdi; David Laird; Maggie Lawrie; Vanessa Loughlin; Aislinn McKibbin; Louise Makin; Geoff Mead; Stephen Moss; Steve Mostyn; Swag Mukerji; Richard Olivier; Sue Page; Iain Perkins; Joyce Redfearn; Claire Reffin; David Robinson; Andrew Ross; Helena Rubinstein; Adrian Simpson; Sue Smith; Philip Sorensen; Andy Sutton; Neill Thomas; Kyle Whitehill; Yasmin Waljee.

Special thanks to Martin Liu, Pom Somkabcharti, and Linette Tye at Cyan Books for all their support.

The following sources provided invaluable material to accompany us on our journeys:

Chapter 1

How to think like Leonardo Da Vinci: Michael Gelb (Thorsons, 1998)

Chapter 4

Managing Talent: Roger Cartwright (Capstone, 2003)

Chapter 6

The Story of English: Robert McCrum, Robert MacNeil, William Cran (Faber and Faber, 1980)

Inspirational Leadership: Henry V and the Muse of Fire: Richard Olivier (Spiro Press, 2002)

Olivier Mythodrama Associates www.oliviermythodrama.com

Small Things that Matter: William Ayot (The Well, 2003)

Chapter 7

Unconditional Leadership: David Robinson (Community Links, 2004)

Fifteen Lessons Learned the Hard Way (FRC Group, 2004)

INTRODUCTION

TODAY people in business have too little time to learn, or at least that's how it seems. Whatever job you do, you are likely to be working at a hectic pace and experiencing unrelenting pressure to deliver more, better, faster. As many of today's professionals are discovering, it seems that no matter how hard you work, there will always be other people who work harder or make themselves and their achievements more visible. In this ferocious competition of talent, how can you consider taking time off to learn? It's a bit like a motor race where everyone believes that taking a pit stop could lose them the race. Attending training courses and conferences and following programs of professional study are all worthwhile. But they require commitment that often involves taking more than a pit stop; rather, you have to be prepared to miss a race or two.

I am not about to argue that it is never worthwhile to take time off the job to learn. Racing drivers do off-the-job training. It takes more than practice laps and natural ability to enable Michael Schumacher, the current Formula 1 champion, to handle the physical and psychological stresses of modern motor racing. A Formula 1 car accelerates from 0 to 160 kph in less than four seconds. It can travel one kilometer from a standing start in 12 seconds, which is roughly five times faster than a normal passenger car. When racing at 160 kph, its braking systems enable it to stop completely in less than two seconds. When this happens, up to 4 G are measured: that is, the driver's body is forced into the seatbelt with four times his or her own weight. The pulse rate of a racing driver reflects the stresses faced. In the pits as he prepares for the race, his resting pulse averages around 60 beats per minute (bpm). As he enters the cockpit, it rises to 90 and during the warm-up lap it reaches 110. Training enables top drivers to hold a pulse rate of 130 as the race starts. Then the body takes over and as they head into the first corner, the pulse can race up to 180. On the Monaco circuit the outer edges of the track do not have any gravel traps, just walls and crash barriers. This pushes stress levels right up and the driver's pulse to a peak of 210 bpm.

To enable him to manage the stresses involved in the 18 championship races held across four continents in a season, a Formula 1 driver will work with a professional fitness trainer. The greater a driver's endurance, the lower his pulse rate and therefore the easier he can deal with the stress. Drivers also work with sports psychologists to learn how to improve their concentration and control their emotions better, for example, in response to making a mistake or annoyance at themselves or another driver.

For most of us taking time out to learn means less time in the driving seat. The result is that we have too little time to learn, develop, and reinvigorate ourselves. This is true of everyone with the will to succeed including school leavers, college graduates, entrepreneurs, managers, aspiring leaders, and established business executives. Unlike racing drivers, businessmen and women may not get to choose the race they are competing in. Worse still, the rules change, often during the race, and what makes people winners today can undermine their success tomorrow. In short, today's business people operate in an increasingly ambiguous, unpredictable, and uncertain world where staying on top means they can't afford to take much time out.

In your own career, it is inevitable that you will have to take some time out of the driving seat to get the training that is specific to your profession or specialism. This is most common early in a career when you are acquiring qualifications and meeting prescribed standards of professional competency. It may also be necessary when you start working with new techniques or methods. Regulation of some industries also requires companies to provide employees with prescribed formal training in certain areas. There are, however, other ways to increase your professional and managerial capability that do not require you to take much time off the job. You may have heard about these and indeed may have experienced them. These include coaching, mentoring, action learning, and project-based learning. In recent years there has been a move away from formal training. Companies have encouraged staff to direct their own learning, by encouraging them to define what new skills and knowledge they need and then providing access to a wide range of resources. These include Internet-based material, which they can follow while working at their desks.

An important underlying principle of this approach is that development is a continuing journey on which you learn to broaden and deepen your capability as a professional and a manager. As a developer, this is a principle that I hold dear and seek to apply in business. It is also one of the principles that have influenced this book. Another is that everyone should have opportunities to fulfil their potential. I recognize that you need the support of others to do this, including partners, bosses, colleagues, coaches, teachers and parents.

So the emphasis of this book is on what you can do for yourself and how you can *be*, which will enable you to take advantage of the learning opportunities that are all around as you go about your daily lives.

My purpose, therefore, in writing this book is to help you fulfill your potential in whatever fields you choose.

My vision: to help you enjoy the benefits of discovering, in every aspect of your life, valuable learnings which are expanding as you become bolder and more curious.

My mission: to stimulate you to explore new aspects of life and discover learning in everything you do.

My role: to act as your guide as we visit new places together and encourage you to see new possibilities in familiar places.

1
DISCOVERY

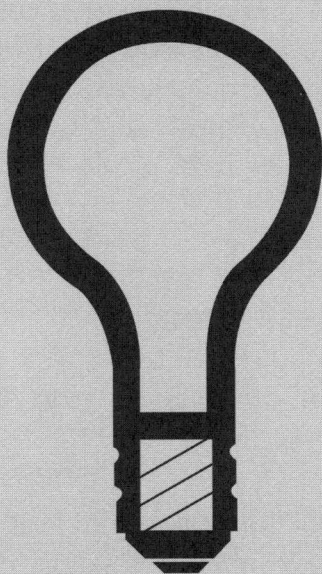

A high-yield, low-risk investment opportunity!

You have all invested valuable time, money and energy to get to where you are in your career today. And you need to be confident that any future investments yield returns that make them worthwhile. So as you take on more responsibility in work and outside, those investments carry higher costs. These include lost time and opportunities in business and lost time with friends and family. I am talking primarily here about investments in formal education and training that require time spent away from the job and possibly home. They may also require you to devote personal time to professional learning, which reduces opportunities for leisure and recreation. There is also the question of whether you are likely to learn more in formal training courses or in other ways. Much research in the area of professional development suggests that while training courses have a role to play, they are only one solution.

We learn best when:

- O we have clear goals and face meaningful challenges

- O we have information that helps us gain insights about how we can develop

- O our bosses actively support our development.

There is therefore a wide range of activities beyond formal training that we can engage in that better meet these requirements. As you read in the introduction, the purpose of this book is to stimulate and guide you to discover how you can deepen and broaden your capabilities, through a minimal investment of additional time, effort and money. These investments will offer considerable returns, whether you measure them in career progression, job satisfaction or a better work–life balance.

This probably reads to you like one of those adverts in the financial pages of the newspaper for:

HIGHLY ATTRACTIVE INVESTMENT OPPORTUNITY, NOT TO BE MISSED

You may think this low-cost, high-reward personal development scheme is just too good to be true. You may want to challenge how I can be so confident that it works. My confidence comes from hearing the stories of the many successful people I interviewed during my research, and from my own experience of working with businessmen and women as a consultant, coach, and executive across a wide range of international companies.

When you read the stories told by these people in this book, you will realize that you are already doing many of the things that are required to make these investments. That is the first piece of good news! The second is that many of you hardly need do much more at all. Rather you need to take a different approach and perhaps put in a bit more effort to take the returns that are there to be harvested, like low-hanging fruit. For others, you may decide to do more of something you are already doing, realizing what great benefits can be had. You may also decide to invest your time and perhaps some money in new activities, with your confidence boosted following your rewarding experiences of initial investments in other areas.

As you read this now, you are probably asking:

- "So what are these investments he is talking about?"

- "What are these stories about?"

- "What is he advising me to do?"

The answers are simple. In this book you will read about successful people discovering learning in unexpected places, and as you read you will discover learnings too. I have found that the more successful people are, the better they are at discovery. They transfer their learnings into their working lives, helping them become more effective professionals and business leaders. They are best at discovery because they think about the way they lead their lives in a different way to most people. Their lives beyond work are an important source of their learning.

That brings me to the third piece of good news. You already spend time in these places! You all have lives outside work. In everything you do outside work there is potential for learning. So in that sense, the places you read about in this book are places most people would expect to be when, for example, they are playing or watching sport or going to the cinema or the concert hall. What is unexpected is that business people can gain learnings from these activities that they successfully apply in their professional lives.

Who are these people? The stories in this book are told by people who work in private and public-sector organizations. They are all successful, holding positions of responsibility in substantial organizations. Some are CEOs, others are managers, and a few are major shareholders of very large companies. None are what could be described as "celebrity businesspeople." The experiences of "celebrities" wouldn't be from unexpected places as their profiles are regularly featured in the pages of business journals and business sections of newspapers. All the people who have told their stories in this book share an openness to new ideas and the flexibility to apply the lessons gained in other parts of their lives to their work.

Learning in unexpected places

Where are the places? They are all around you. They are the types of places that we all go to as we engage in the diverse range of activities that make up our lives. The things we do there, whether it is watching a movie or television program, playing or watching sport, listening to music, playing an instrument, or spending time with our families, offer a rich source of learning.

What will you learn?

You will discover that as you read the stories and also reflect on your own experiences inside and outside of work.

How will you learn?

You all learn in different ways and at different levels. Some of the stories clearly describe how someone was inspired by something they learnt from, for example, playing a sport then systematically applying their insights to deliver impressive results in business. Others will tell you how they were inspired by watching a film or a play or listening to a poetry reading.

In conducting my research for this book, I found that very few people had discovered learnings across a very wide range of activities. It was most common for people to discover learning in only one or two places, even if they participated in a wide range of activities. Some people were inspired by aspects of their lives outside work but couldn't describe at all the impact it had on their professional life. Why is that? It is easy to answer. "because we are all different." It may be that some people inevitably are better discoverers. Their approach is more conducive to learning and their practice of the disciplines of discovery is better.

As we visit the unexpected places that I have chosen for our journey together, you will realize how everyday conversations are learning opportunities. People like you find valuable lessons in unexpected places, often close to home, by knowing how and where to look. We all have access to the places where learning can be discovered unexpectedly. I suspect some people rarely visit them. Others go there and the opportunities pass them by. Many are inspired yet don't translate this inspiration into learning that changes the way they do their work. A substantial and growing number do discover learning in unexpected places that changes the way they are working for the better. This journey that we take together will encourage you to make more discoveries.

Be bold. Visit more places and with a curiosity of spirit. Be more receptive to new ideas. Seek more to understand. Enquire more. Take some risks. Experiment. Try out things and challenge your assumptions about what works how, where, and why. You will find it very rewarding.

You will only fulfill your potential if you tap into your potential for learning, continually discovering new and better ways of doing things and generating and sustaining the momentum that is the lifeblood of personal and commercial success. This need to learn and develop goes beyond simply acquiring knowledge and skills. It is also about acquiring confidence, increasing awareness, clarifying direction, and maintaining a receptiveness to challenge, leading to new insights and growth.

I invite you now, beginning as you read this book, to embark daily on your own adventures of discovery, to learn in unexpected places and enjoy the rewards of your journey as you fulfill your potential in your chosen field whether a specific profession, corporate career, as an entrepreneur, or some other calling.

What is discovery?

> Discovery is:
>
> - driven by curiosity
>
> - illuminated by insight
>
> - realized through focused application.

It is a way of being, an attitude, and an approach that can differentiate you from your peers. Discovery enables you to make the most of the conditions for effective development when:

- you have clear goals and face meaningful challenges

- you have information that helps to gain insights about how you can develop

- your bosses actively support your development.

Discovery enables you to fulfill your potential to perform roles where you will deliver extraordinary results. In the words of mathematician, Henri Poincaré, "It is by logic you prove, but by intuition that you discover." When you practice discovery, your curiosity leads you to places not immediately relevant to your current professional and personal world. Gaining insights there, your awareness is raised about how you can become truly outstanding in your chosen field. Focusing your learning on what is important, you realize the benefits both in your career and personal life.

Discovery is driven by curiosity, seeking new situations to explore or wanting to know more about what is familiar. The curious professional will seek new experiences, read new books, watch new movies, listen to new music, and do new things. We are born with the drive to be curious: to see, hear, feel, smell, and taste new things, and to understand what lies behind these sensations for our fellow human beings and ourselves. Children are often warned, "Your curiosity will lead you into trouble." I am sure this is true of many children. It is also true that the curiosity of millions of children has enabled them to discover experiences and the joys associated with them, as well as talents that they did not realize they had.

Without curiosity you will limit yourself to what is familiar. You will stay in your comfort zone. You won't travel far and when you do it will be by familiar means. Our natural curiosity has been the source of the progress of humankind over the centuries. Developments in medicine, science, technology, arts, and literature were only possible because our forefathers were prepared to enquire and had the courage to venture forth where their fathers before them had not. In the words of André Gide: "One does not discover new lands without consenting to lose sight of the shore for a very long time."

A great way to learn is by observing people who are masters in their field, exemplars of their craft. Aspiring leaders are exhorted in leadership development literature to find someone who they admire, a person who role models the attributes they believe essential for success. Many chose a much-admired senior executive in their own firm, but you needn't be restricted to your current organization when seeking a role model. You don't even need to restrict yourself to business, nor do you need to restrict yourself to the present time. So in the spirit of losing sight of the shore for a while, I will encourage you to travel back in time to Renaissance Europe and consider Leonardo da Vinci as a role model.

His curiosity led him to accomplish so much, as a painter, architect, engineer, anatomist, mathematician, and philosopher, that he has been acclaimed by many as the greatest genius of all time. Michael Gelb describes Leonardo as the "supreme global archetype of human potential who represents our capacities more completely than anyone who ever walked the earth." Leonardo was intensely curious about his environment. He kept a notebook so that he could write ideas and impressions as they happened. The following quote from one of his notebooks shows how his curiosity embraced the natural world as he experienced it, as well as his formal studies:

> I roamed the countryside searching for answers to things I did not understand. Why shells existed on the tops of mountains along with imprints of coral, plants and seaweed usually found in the sea. Why the thunder lasts a longer time than that which causes it and why immediately on its creation the lightning becomes visible to the eye, while thunder requires time to travel. How the various circles of water form around the spot which has been struck by a stone, and why a bird sustains itself in the air. These questions and other strange phenomena engage my thought throughout my life.

Leonardo's discoveries were driven by such curiosity, as will your discoveries as you adopt this questioning approach to your daily life. You will broaden your experiences, creating the opportunity to deepen your understanding and increase your own capacity as a human being, as a professional, as a leader.

The importance of application

While curiosity is essential, it is not sufficient for discovery. You could argue that whilst the questions asked by Leonardo were a reflection of his wisdom, he could not have accomplished what he did solely by asking questions. The seeking of the answer is only the beginning of discovery. The development of insight that flows from the questioning is the critical next step. To be able to tell a story, the people we meet in the places we visit together in this book had to be curious. They had to watch the movie, play the game, listen to the music, and they had to ask themselves and others questions about their experiences. To gain insights you have to be prepared to challenge your own and others' assumptions about why and how things are the way they are. It is this challenging of assumptions that is critical, reflecting an unwillingness to accept opinion. You have to test understanding through a combination of analysis and experience; welcoming the perspective of others and being prepared to learn from your own and others' mistakes.

Having gained insights, discovery can only be realized through application.

Enlightenment has its own intrinsic value, but its contribution to our lives requires application of knowledge. Making connections is fundamental to this. When we make connections, for example, we understand why a character in the movie felt betrayed by her friend and what then happened to their relationship. Having played in an orchestra, I know how the conductor behaves when he gets us all to play in harmony with each other. It's clear too how my teammates in my volleyball team behave when we play at our best. Understanding the "how" opens up the possibility of transferring that learning to another area of activity. Recognizing the patterns of behavior in one sphere of life offers the possibility of applying them in another, and that is what many of the people we will meet do. Translating understanding gained in one place and applying it to their business or other aspects of their lives takes courage, confidence, and a willingness to make mistakes. But it is not the making of mistakes that matters. Rather it's what you do as a result of making mistakes that makes the difference. It's what you do with the insight gained that enables you to practice discovery.

In the next section of this book I will act as your guide as we visit several places. Some are familiar and others will be new to you. As we travel we will meet fascinating people, and you will hear their stories of how they benefit from this approach by demonstrating a willingness to explore new experiences, becoming aware of the learnings offered, having the imagination and discipline to translate this learning into action, and possessing an enduring spirit of curiosity that sustains their momentum for continual growth and development.

Unexpected places

Having introduced you to discovery, we will now explore together some unexpected places. You will meet people like yourself who work in organizations, and you will realize how the places they visit yield valuable learning that can be transferred to their work-places and other aspects of their lives.

In planning this program of visits for you, I had many stimu-lating and rewarding conversations with business people about the unexpected places where they learn. First I asked a group of business executives and professionals to describe the impact that their hobbies and interests outside work had on their business and professional lives. I was particularly interested in how these activities were a source of learning for them. For example, partic-ipating in their hobby may inspire them to do something they would not have otherwise done, prompt them to do something differently, influence an important decision, or deepen their understanding of a challenging situation.

To discover what these places have to offer, I now invite you to join me on this journey.

2
CINEMA

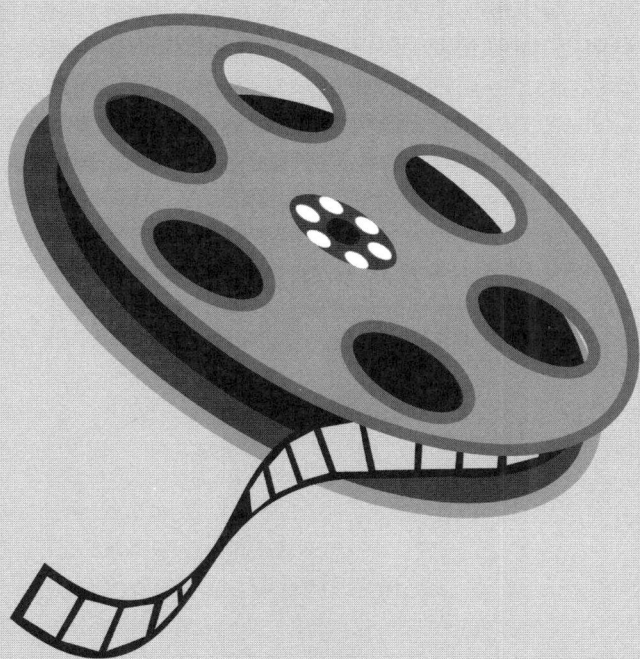

THE FIRST PLACE I am taking you to is the cinema. It is not far to travel, and like most cinemas now it is a multiplex, showing several films at one time. But as we drive closer, you can see the program, and there is something unusual about it. This cinema is showing an unusual collection. Normally it would list new or recent releases, but although some of the films are fairly recent, others are old. One was made 30 years ago, another over 60 years ago, and there are a couple of television shows. You won't have seen the film version of these TV shows. They were never made into films so it might seem strange to see them listed like this. It is unusual, rather special, something I've arranged. It will all become clear very soon. Look at the listings:

DISCOVERY CINEMA

NOW SHOWING

GANDHI

a film by Richard Attenborough,
starring Ben Kingsley

✩✩✩

ZELIG

Starring Woody Allen

✩✩✩

THE BRIDGE (Die Bruecke)

✩✩✩

THEY DIED WITH THEIR BOOTS ON

starring Errol Flynn & Olivia de Havilland

✩✩✩

JERRY MAGUIRE

starring Tom Cruise

✩✩✩

THE GODFATHER

starring Marlon Brando

✩✩✩

THE FIRM

starring Tom Cruise

✩✩✩

THE OFFICE

with Ricky Gervais

✩✩✩

HILL STREET BLUES

Nine films in one evening? Impossible? Wrong. I've arranged a special evening at the cinema for you. We will be meeting some friends who have selected parts of these films and television programs to show us. They will talk with us about why they are special to them and what they have learnt from them.

As we enter the cinema complex, we are shown into a theater. It is much smaller than you would normally expect. The screen takes up the whole of the wall facing us, and you can imagine that when the film is showing it seems like you are right there at that place in time. Waiting to greet us are eight men and a woman. I introduce everyone, and we sit down in the comfortable sofas with a drink in our hands, and wait with anticipation for the lights to go down . Andy, one of our friends, explains that we are now going to see a special program of excerpts from movies that they have had made for us at my request. After each one, the projector will pause and our friends will take a few minutes to talk with us about it.

The lights go down.

The first clip we see is from Richard Attenborough's *Gandhi,* which describes how one man's personal beliefs can transform a nation's politics. We see the young Gandhi, working as a solicitor, being thrown off a train in South Africa because he refuses to be bullied out of a first-class carriage for which he has purchased a ticket. First class was barred to blacks and colored people in those days. We then see him travel by boat to India where the Indian people were oppressed, suffering prejudice just because of the color of their skin. There was much violence, yet Gandhi's response was peaceful, non-violent and non-cooperative. It was powerfully symbolic and there was not much the British could do to counter him.

There is a scene at a salt works that is a great example of the power of his philosophy of civil disobedience. The British had a monopoly on the manufacture of salt. It was very important. We hear a British official say: "In India, nothing lives without salt. Our control of salt manufacture is the control on the pulse of India."

Responding to British insistence that all salt manufacture must be licensed and taxed, Gandhi embarks on a 240-mile march from his birthplace in Porbandar to the sea. He arrives there on the anniversary of the Amritsar massacre in which over 1500 peacefully protesting Indians were shot by the British Army. He openly defies the law by making salt. People all over India follow his example and make salt illegally. The British react, arresting 100,000 salt makers including Gandhi. In a further act of defiance, thousands of Indian protestors march peacefully to the Dharasana Salt Works. The factory is closed, and guards stand barring the way, threatening to hit the protestors. As the first person is knocked down, the next one takes his place. An American journalist, who has just observed the brutal treatment of the peaceful protestors, is shown filing his story with these words: "Today whatever moral ascendancy the West held has gone."

The lights go up and Swag, who is financial director of a healthcare company, describes the impact that Attenborough's film had on him:

> I watched this movie with my parents, who were both born in India, trained as doctors and subsequently emigrated to UK. It was their era. My father was 17 at the time and was just about to go to university. He saw it as an accurate depiction of the time.

Swag describes how watching the movie influenced his approach to business:

> Whenever I am about to go head to head, I take time to understand the competition's strengths and weaknesses then devise my strategy accordingly. I previously ran a soft drinks company and we were trying to take market share from a major competitor, which was very large and very inflexible. They provided fridges in small shops on

condition that only their products were stocked in them. They were very regimented and would always visit shops every six weeks. We came in after them and gave the shopkeeper our product free if they would put it in the fridge. Nobody wants to buy warm cola. We also visited the shops more frequently, and as a result took major market share gains from them.

Gandhi helped Swag realize the importance of understanding your own strengths in relation to your business competitors, creatively devising a strategy that plays to your strengths, undermines your competitors, and has the element of surprise. Following Gandhi's philosophy he devised something they had never before encountered and did not know how to deal with.

The lights go down and we are now watching Woody Allen's 1983 film, *Zelig*. Woody plays the title character, Leonard Zelig. His co-star is Mia Farrow who plays Dr. Eudora Fletcher, the psychiatrist who takes charge of Zelig's case when he is admitted to hospital. Leonard Zelig is a character who apparently has no beliefs or opinions of his own. He simply adopts the norms of those around him. He is so keen to please, to conform, that he turns into the person he is with. Not only does he assume their values, he is also physically transformed, adopting their ethnic characteristics, body shape, facial hair, and costumes. We see him as a gangster, black jazz musician, Scotsman, and alongside Adolf Hitler at a Nazi rally and Pope Pius at the Vatican.

This film was chosen for us by Neill, who is a partner in a financial services firm. He first saw it in 1983 when he was a student. Whereas Swag's lessons were primarily about dealing with competitors, this film helped Neill develop some insights about managing relationships with clients and colleagues.

He was amused by the film but recognized that through extreme exaggeration, it warned of the dangers of seeking too close a rapport with clients and colleagues:

Nobody would want to emulate Leonard Zelig. The film was light hearted enough, but there is no doubt that clients gravitate towards people with whom they feel comfortable. By definition these will be people closest to their own character. I have found myself often adapting my style when dealing with a client. Recently I was doing a pitch to a prospective client. He was very quiet, keeping his cards close to his chest. I noticed myself quietening my voice, steadying my pitch, responding. It is interesting how you are more comfortable with people who are like you. Recalling that movie heightened my awareness of the importance of being in tune with clients and colleagues but the dangers of taking it too far and subsuming one's own personality and values as Zelig did.

The way that Zelig suppresses his own identity to fit in with others seems ridiculous, but it does have sinister overtones. The film does provide a warning about the risk of too much compliance with the prevailing values of other individuals and organization culture.

Next we hear from Markus who was born and brought up in Germany. He is the communication and engagement manager for a global energy corporation. His choice of film is no surprise given the role he performs in business. It is *The Bridge* (*Die Bruecke*). Made in 1959, it is a German film and provides Markus with strong lessons about the power and responsibilities of communication.

The lights go down again and we see the story of seven school-boys who are drafted in 1945 as Germany moved towards defeat. Their wise schoolteacher tries to safeguard the lives of his pupils by arranging for them to guard a bridge that is of no consequence and is going to be blown up anyway. As the Americans approach the town where they live, they do not expect it to draw heavy bombardment. The boys are not aware of this, and one of them is the son of a high-ranking German army officer. As the Americans approach, he convinces his schoolmates that they must (need-lessly) defend the bridge. As a result, they stay at their posts even after German soldiers retreat across it . The consequence is that all but two of the class are killed, and the village draws heavy bombardment with many lives lost. When German soldiers eventually arrive to blow up the bridge, the surviving boys then realize that their friend's deaths were completely in vain, and fire on their own countrymen.

Markus sums up for us the impact on him: "The lesson for me is how important it is to use your powers of influence and communication judiciously and from a sound values base when you have the 'power' to exhort others to action."

The 1942 action-packed *They Died with their Boots On* is the choice of Allan, a senior executive in a financial services company. You have probably seen it more than once, on television on a wet Sunday afternoon. The stars are Errol Flynn as General George Custer and Olivia de Havilland as Elizabeth Bacon. It is the story of Custer from his time at West Point Military Academy, through the Civil War, to his defeat by Chief Crazy Horse at the battle of Little Big Horn.

Allan highlights the power of symbolic action by Custer, which easily translates to business:

> It is the overall feel of the film that appeals. Taking soldiers in a mess and transforming them. Custer finds a fort full of drunken oafs and forges them into a fighting unit. There is a point where Custer shuts down the bar. The soldiers are speechless and then they realize he was right. He had symbolized the start of a new era, the start of change. In business life, at times you have to be cruel to be kind. You have to make changes that will have an adverse impact on some individuals for the greater good of the organization. When I took over a new team some time ago, there was an individual who was very popular and had hitherto been

very successful. His performance had deteriorated and he was unwilling to respond to coaching. We eventually parted company and I heard soon after that my action had sent waves around the organization. An influential figure in another department commented that my action was symbolic that the company would now change. I brought in a replacement who has been a resounding success and role model for the new way of doing business.

In our next film Tom Cruise plays the title role in *Jerry Maguire* (1996), a character who is committed to changing the way his firm does business. This is the first of two films featuring Tom Cruise in our program. Michael, who is chief operating officer of a global satellite communications firm, has selected this film for you.

Michael describes *Jerry Maguire* as:

> … an inspiring film with an underlying message that it's worth sticking to something you passionately believe in, even if there are unpleasant consequences on the journey to realising your end goal.

"Show me the money, Jerry," demands Ron Tidwell. Ron, played by Cuba Gooding Jr, is a football player and client of Jerry Maguire. Jerry is an account manager for a firm promoting the interests of sports stars and celebrities. He is enthusing about the virtues of his new personalized service for clients, but Ron wants to know what is really in it for him and whether it offers any real value.

There are other lessons in this film, which Michael draws out:

> "Show me the money" is a quote that I have used on many occasions when reviewing sales prospect pipelines, business cases, and new service ideas. It's a very simple way of getting people to think about the quantitative outcomes of their activities, efforts, and ideas. I have

used this mindset to positive effect at current and previous companies to challenge investment proposals and focus on returns and outcomes.

In stark contrast to Woody Allen's Zelig, Jerry Maguire has a strong sense of his own identity and values. Michael says:

> Jerry is very courageous. He has a conviction about how his firm can provide better service to clients and is inspired to produce a mission statement which he publicises and distributes to colleagues. His mission comes from deep within. He challenges his sense of purpose. Asks himself who he has become. Is he just another shark in a suit? So he begins writing a mission statement … to say it out loud. He describes it as putting yourself out there naked. But his mission doesn't go down well. His boss doesn't like it and fires Jerry. Ron Tidwell is the only client that stays with Jerry initially. He hangs in and eventually he is inundated by new clients.

It's a powerful, optimistic story where a man with the courage of his convictions prevails in the end.

Francis Ford Coppola's *The Godfather* (1972) is arguably one of the greatest films of all time, and Chris, sales director of a software company, selects a scene that provides, for him, a perfect summary of stakeholder management. He explains:

> I'll never forget the advice given by Don Corleone (Marlon Brando) to his son, Michael (Al Pacino) to "Keep your friends close, but your enemies closer."
>
> We see Corleone early in the film advising his son about the importance of talking to people outside the family. We have a natural tendency to spend time with people we like and avoid those we don't. It's not really

about good guys and bad guys. In any organization, there will always be conflicts of interest. Rather than struggle with this we often try to work with people we like. We need to talk to those we think we have less in common with, to ensure they don't damage our business goals and that they understand what we want and vice versa.

Chris tells us how he followed the Don's advice to good effect in his current company.

The strategy director had different ideas about the direction of the group than I had. As I spent much time in the U.S., I discovered there wasn't much happening there and what was happening wasn't appropriate. We were both pursuing different agendas. We did not trust each other. He thought I was resisting him because he was on my patch. The more time I spent with him, I began to appreciate that he wasn't attached to a specific agenda but he needed to demonstrate progress. The more I pushed my agenda, the more he pushed his. He was responsible for the U.S. because he was global strategy director. I had a management role with resources and power and I was based in the U.S. We put together a team, working on development, discussed options, and came up with a strategy that we could both commit to.

So by following the advice of the Godfather, Chris developed a relationship with someone he thought was his enemy and they became effective allies.

The importance of being true to yourself is a strong theme of another film that has provided important lessons for a business executive. Andy is vice president of a global software company, and the next film we see and discuss is *The Firm (1993)*, which is our second featuring Tom Cruise.

We see Tom Cruise playing Mitch McDeere, an outstanding Harvard law graduate. He is courted by many prestigious legal firms, and joins a firm in Memphis, which offers a salary far in excess of all the others. In addition, they provide him and his wife with a house and luxury car. They even pay off his student loan, and it seems too good to be true, as Mitch eventually realizes it is. There are some early indications that "the firm" will seek to influence their private lives. Mitch's wife is asked if she plans to have children and colleagues' wives tell her the firm encourages children. They express surprise when she continues working. All lawyers there are male and none have ever been divorced. The firm encourages stability in the domestic lives of its partners and staff.

From his first day Mitch finds himself overloaded. He is working all hours, sees less of his family, and starts sleeping in the office. This begins to put strains on his marriage. In addition, things get sinister when two lawyers die violently in mysterious circumstances. He soon discovers he is working for a corrupt firm, with close connections to organized crime and deeply involved in illegal business activities. The erosion of his initial euphoria is complete, and the impact the job has on his marriage and family life is near-disastrous. Through ingenuity, determination, and some good fortune, Mitch rescues his marriage, and manages to slip away from the tentacles of the mob and FBI.

Andy talks about the impact *The Firm* made on him:

> The big lesson for me here is the importance of keeping things in perspective. You can chase the silver dollar but there has to be a healthy balance between this and broader life (your family, kids, health, happiness—which ultimately is far more important) and you have to find a career path in which you can be true to your own principles. Ignore these at your long-term peril.

Now here's where we bent the rules a bit in preparing tonight's show. We are about to see on the big screen some footage that would normally be seen on the small screen.

The lights go down again and we are now watching a scene in a business park in Slough, England, location of Wernham Hogg, the fictitious paper company featured in the BBC sitcom *The Office*. We see Ricky Gervais, as David Brent, the manager. Nobody aspires to emulate him but most suspect that, on occasions, they may have exhibited some of his less desirable traits or certainly know a colleague who has.

Jeff, sales and marketing director of a consumer goods company, tells why *The Office* provides an excellent blueprint of how not to behave in business:

> The episode where they have a training day sums him up. He just won't let go and trust anyone. He gets in a trainer but he's not prepared to let the trainer get on with it. Brent stays with the class and eventually takes it over. He doesn't trust what the staff will say when he's not there. It's a nice cameo of what not to do.

The reaction of Michael who spoke to us about *Jerry Maguire* earlier, is one that you may have experienced when watching Brent stumble clumsily from one faux pas to the next:

> Can anyone have sat through some of the more cringe-worthy scenes in this excellent "docu-comedy" without having actively evaluated their (mis-)use of jargon in the work place and how words and deeds are perceived by colleagues and clients alike? I showed a friend an excerpt of a presentation I'd given at one of our distributor events last year and was disconcerted to have her laugh and claim that my earnest delivery was a little too much, falling into the "David Brent" category. I have actively reviewed my presentations for any sign of apparent

insincerity or faux earnestness since then. Brent's painfully embarrassing behaviour challenges us all to ask ourselves, "Am I being too earnest, too glib?"

For the final item of our program we travel from a business park in Slough, across the Atlantic to a ghetto area of a large unnamed eastern city in the U.S.A. Hill Street Police Station is our next location, where another role model, this time a positive one, awaits us in the form of Captain Frank Furillo. We see this principal character of the 1980s television series *Hill Street Blues* demonstrate his quiet, forceful, and patient qualities, while dealing on a daily basis with an endless flow of undesirables who inhabit his precinct. Anne , global head of people development at a telecommunications company, describes him as*:*

> An excellent role model who always gave perfect feedback: clear rationale, short, at the right time, and unmistakably clear. I used to quote him when I ran management training courses! I also tried to emulate him—but know I failed … [she laughs] I didn't have his team of scriptwriters!

Neither did we have Frank's scriptwriters but we did have a great team of producers who put together a truly inspirational package of video footage conveying some very valuable learning from some unexpected places.

As we leave the cinema, I ask you to consider whether there are times you have watched a film or television show that challenged your thinking in some way or caused you to reflect on situations in your business or personal life. When this happened what did you do as a result? On reflection was there anything that you could have done differently as a result of these discoveries?

3
MUSIC STORE

FOR OUR NEXT outing, I've arranged to take you a music store in a less fashionable part of town. It's one of those stores that you don't come across too often now. Downstairs, they sell musical instruments. In the window there's a baby grand piano. On a rack to the side there are gleaming electric guitars. On the floor stands a full drum kit. Beside it are tom-toms, maracas and tambourines. This is one of the few places in town you can buy sheet music. Upstairs we can hear the sound system and that's where you can find a CD of any music recording that was ever made. If they don't have it in stock, they'll get it in for you really quickly.

It's Saturday afternoon and there are lots of people in the store: teenagers plucking away at the strings of electric guitars; parents pondering the purchase of a piano for their daughter, and other kids just hanging around, soaking up the atmosphere and chatting to friends whilst they listen to the latest releases.

Ode to joy

Towards the side of the shop window, standing parallel to the wall, is an electronic keyboard. On its stand is the sheet music for *Ode to Joy,* and I walk over and pick out the melody with one hand. *Ode to Joy* is from the fourth movement of Beethoven's Ninth or "Choral" Symphony. It reminds me of a story that I heard from David, who is a senior executive with a professional services company. A few years ago he learnt to sing *Ode to Joy* with 750 colleagues when they were entertained after a dinner by Benjamin Zander, conductor of the Boston Philharmonic Orchestra.

Zander had talked to them about motivation, and how he applied his conducting skills to teaching. He described how his students always get top grades. Of course one wonders how this can be, but the psychology he uses is interesting: his students have to write him a letter at the start of term telling how they will get an A grade. It tells him everything he needs to know to get the best out of them.

The event David attended coincided with the fiftieth birthday of one of his colleagues. Somehow Zander got 750 senior executives to sing a pretty impressive happy birthday to Duncan. Amazingly he then got them to make an even better sound by changing the intonation, and finally had them singing *Ode to Joy.* It made a big impression on David.

He had experienced Benjamin Zander apply an important leadership principle: "Never doubt the capacity of the people you lead to accomplish whatever you dream for them." Zander argues that it is a principle that leaders like Gandhi, Martin Luther King Jr, and Nelson Mandela have all embodied. He teased his audience by suggesting: "Imagine if Martin Luther King had said, 'I have a dream—I wonder if people will be up to it?'"

Who is Benjamin Zander? He is a world-renowned conductor. Born in England, he studied there with Benjamin Britten, then trained as a cellist in Florence and Cologne before graduating from London University in 1964. He won a postgraduate scholarship at Harvard and his home has been in Boston ever since. He travels the world conducting, teaching, and lecturing. He has presented at the World Economic Forum in Davos and gives presentations like the one David described to many international corporations.

One of Zander's dreams is that everybody can sing. He is amazed at the number of people who tell him they are tone deaf. He does not believe that anybody is tone deaf, but rather that they were told by someone when they were young that they couldn't sing. Children grow up thinking they can't sing because like many accomplished musicians, they are having what Zander calls the "conversation in the head." He believes that in any performance, there are always two people onstage: the one trying to play and another who whispers: "Do you know how many people can play better than you?" or "Here comes that difficult passage you missed last time … you're going to miss it again!" He warns that sometimes that voice is so loud that it drowns out the music, and that's why he sees his role as a leader, to find ways to silence that voice and to help his musicians, his students, his audiences of business executives realize their capacities to be fully expressive.

The letter Zander gets his students to write, describing what they will do to deserve their A grade, gives him rich information about how the students relate to their dreams. Here are some examples of the type of things they say: "I'm not shy any more," "I now enjoy playing," and "Criticism doesn't get me down any more." This is the type of information that he needs to help them perform at their best.

Classical guitar

David himself became a student of music recently. When he turned 50 he decided to learn the classical guitar. At the outset, his teacher played a beautiful and somewhat complicated Spanish piece (*Recuerdos de la Alhambra*) and suggested to David's amazement that he would be able to play it too. His teacher works on the principle "give a man a fish and you feed him for a day; teach a man how to fish and you'll feed him for life." He took David straight into playing the tune, after some preliminary groundwork.

Here's how David described the impact that his teacher had on him:

> Music can either be very complicated or delightfully simple; learning to play the piano as a child was a chore for me, consisting as it did of boring scales and obscure classical pieces in which I had no real interest. It was taught by rote, and the rules had to be obeyed! I gave up playing the piano, much to my regret later on. Learning to play classical guitar in middle age, and being taught by someone who teaches *how* to play, using his insight to my ability and personal motivation, has taken me to places I had not imagined possible.

Going to places you had not imagined possible. That is true discovery!

There's another David I know who also embarked on a similar journey. He is a divisional director of a pharmaceutical group. He also started playing guitar at 50 and found it a humbling experience, bringing home to him what it was like to be absolutely useless at something. He told me it took him six months to get three chords down and play at will. As a result, he became more tolerant of less experienced staff at the bottom of the learning curve.

David told me he is the type of person who likes things to happen quickly. If he is able to put together a business plan quickly, for example, he will expect similar standards from whomever he has delegated it to. He admitted that anything he does well, he tends to think others should be able to as well. But everything you do, you have to learn. When he reflected on this insight, he thought about situations where perhaps he had been too hard. Here he describes the insight he discovered as a result of learning a new musical instrument in middle age:

> It is a learning curve, not a spike. You need to make mistakes at the bottom of the curve to get up there. You learn most of your skills early and as you get older, there is less you have to learn. It doesn't mean you stop learning or don't need to keep learning as you get older. Your foundation skills as a professional, though, the things you must learn to do your job satisfactorily, are acquired early. It is easy to forget that it took you time to learn. When I saw the first draft of a business plan produced by a subordinate I thought, oh God, I'll have to do it myself. But then I realized it would be far better to coach the individual what and how to do it, and I did. I gained an important lesson about how I can manage people better, as a result of challenges I faced in my leisure.

What a coincidence! Two men deciding at the same point in their lives to start playing the same musical instrument. In the process they both discovered powerful lessons about how they learn themselves and how they can be more effective in supporting others to learn.

The samba

The store is getting busier now, as the afternoon moves on and I notice how many different percussion instruments there are: big floor drums, cymbals, bongos, tambourines, maracas, cowbells, shakers, and triangles. They probably stock so many because they are popular with young school children. If you're like me, one of the first instruments you ever played was in a junior school band, shaking a shaker or banging a tambourine. Percussion instruments always appeal, with their pleasing, unusual shapes, but they are deceptive. There's much more to them than picking them up and striking them spontaneously. I have to admit that I have often been disappointed by the results when trying to play percussion.

That contrasts with the experience of many people who have learned to play percussion with an outfit called BeatsWork who specialize in teambuilding. Paul Brown from BeatsWork is a professional percussionist who introduces large groups of novices to the samba, and within two hours they are transformed: playing the instruments in harmony, in time, and on cue.

Before I tell you some more about Paul and the samba, let me pause for a moment and ask you a question. What do you do when you are merging five sales teams? Getting them together banging drums and bashing a load of percussion instruments would not be the obvious thing to do when faced with such a daunting business challenge. But that is exactly the path followed by Kyle, sales director of a mobile phone company. You may be wondering why this experience was so relevant to Kyle's challenge.

Paul's approach mirrors the journey that Kyle would be taking with his team. The large group is divided into small teams, and they go off into separate rooms with their own percussion teacher. They learn very quickly the basics of the samba rhythms, playing a plethora of instruments, including snare drums, kettle-drums, floor drums, cymbals, tambourines, triangles, cowbells, and shakers. They learn how to keep time, reading audio and

43

visual signals for "breaks" (changes in rhythm). Having mastered their individual skills within small teams, they all merge together to deliver an awe-inspiring performance as one large integrated team. They play in harmony with a common purpose, enjoying a shared sense of achievement.

Kyle described to me the impact of this experience with his people:

> Bringing 256 people from five separate teams together, I wanted to emphasize that the whole was greater than the sum of the original parts. We arranged a conference. After lunch, the room was cleared. The purpose of the session was to energize us, get us working as one, realizing that if we were to get better we needed to rely on each other. Paul split us into several small groups and this was a great bonding session, learning in those small units. The experience made a huge impact on us. It helped us get off to a great start, and we have gone from strength to strength since."

What makes this experience so powerful and relevant to people in organizations? There are similarities in the challenges people face in business to those in becoming musicians in a samba band: the need to learn and acquire new skills and knowledge quickly; to work together effectively; to play in harmony, knowing when to be forceful and when to allow others to take the lead; and the focus on results, delivering a performance that will exceed expectations. All those elements are present in the BeatsWork experience. So is that it? Is there more to it than the fact that it is a very cleverly designed exercise that provides a metaphor for the demanding performance challenges of today's business?

Paul Brown believes the power of the samba experience is in the spirit of the music. He has taught samba to business executives all over the world, working with groups up to 1500 with a team of 30 teachers. His view is that it enhances belief in oneself and colleagues. Participants are so pleasantly surprised at what they are able to achieve. He often receives comments like: "We didn't believe we could do it" and "We've learnt so much in such a short time." Paul says that the importance of communication is the strongest theme emerging with clients.

To discover what is special about the spirit of samba, we need to travel back to its roots. In the nineteenth century, African slaves brought their native music and dance to Brazil. This combined with the European traditions of carnivals, balls and parades creating the spectacular Brazilian carnival extravaganza. Paul himself has performed in Carnival in São Paulo. What struck him was the central part that it played in people's lives, particularly the poor. Many of whom contribute to savings clubs all year long to be able to buy their "fantasy," as the extravagant costumes are known. He had a full day of 'training' in preparation for his samba school's 4 a.m. slot on the Sambadroma. This large broad corridor extends several hundred meters and is flanked by terraced seating, through which each school of several hundred people parades before the judges. Paul remembers a man standing on top of a bus as he was entering the Sambadroma, expressing extravagant expectations of the whole phenomenon that were not untypical. He shouted, "You gotta be ready to die for the samba."

The costumes, the parading, the showing off, the glamor, the spontaneity, all excite the child within, enabling us to experience real joy. The essence of that spirit carried in the samba rhythms recreates for business executives many thousands of miles away enough of that atmosphere to release that inner child love of learning deep within. It stimulates the courage to take a risk, try something new, and experience real joy at accomplishment beyond our expectations.

I'll leave the last word on samba to an executive from Aon Corporation. He had experienced BeatsWork with Paul, and a few weeks later was meeting with a professor from a prestigious business school to discuss an assignment. The aim was to clarify the business strategy and align the team behind it. The professor began describing his approach, which model he would use, and what techniques would be appropriate. The executive looked impatient and interrupted:

> Let me tell you what we are looking for. A month ago we had this musician come in and split us into groups. We were learning how to play musical instruments. We only had an hour and we were getting worried that soon we would have to get up on stage and be good enough to compete with all the other groups. But that didn't happen. Instead we all got back into the large hall and he stood up on stage and all 100 of us played, together, in harmony. That's the result I want to achieve.

That's the power of the samba experience!

More and more people now are drifting upstairs in the store as the music gets louder, and I decided we should go up and have a look. It is darker upstairs and it's difficult to hear each other speaking as we move through the rows of CDs. I also notice there is a specialist section on vinyl, which has become a cult fashion now that hardly anybody has a turntable.

Whenever I go into music shops I spend some time looking for CDs of music that I have heard recently, and stuff that was popular when I was young but that I haven't got at home. We browse through the categories and reach the punk section. There it is, a CD of an album I never bought in the late 1970s when it was released, *Never Mind the Bollocks* by the Sex Pistols. Looking over the cover at the song titles, I think to myself, I never ever did get around to buying it and I never will. I never thought it was any good then and nothing will ever change my mind.

Swag who is financial director of a healthcare company would not argue with me much about the Sex Pistols' musical talent. But he does admit to drawing learning from the attitude of the musicians rather than the music itself. He explains:

> The Sex Pistols weren't talented musically, but they had lots

of attitude. They demonstrated that, even if you don't have outstanding talent, you should never believe that you can't have success. It's all in the mind. [The] Sex Pistols changed the rules of music. At the time the fashion was for big stadium concerts, they created small concerts in small venues. Self-belief and determination was the key to their success.

Swag applied this attitude in a previous company:

> Our technical experts believed our product was not good enough and therefore nobody would buy it. They were looking for perfection. I used the example of The Sex Pistols with colleagues. They weren't that good but nobody else was doing what they were doing. Just because you don't think it's perfect doesn't mean other people won't put a value on it. It's all about getting people to believe in themselves.

Self-belief and determination, two good notes to leave on as we complete our visit to the music store.

4
SPORTS CLUB

EVERYONE PARTICIPATES in some sporting activity in their life, even if for some of us it is under duress at school. Many are enthusiastic, and most who have played a sport have dreamt of sporting greatness. Perhaps it was momentarily when everything went right and you scored that goal, made that pass, hit that shot, made that tackle that was perfect. Perhaps one day, I can be … a champion, a hero, a heroine. The dreams fade for most of us, but to be a truly great sporting champion you must keep it alive, to desire it passionately and dedicate yourself to live out your dream. In the summer of 2004 in Athens, British athlete Kelly Holmes achieved an amazing feat, at the age of 34, winning double gold medals in the women's 800 and 1500 meters. When interviewed on television immediately after the race, she proclaimed: "I've dreamt about this every day of my athletics career."

Kelly admitted afterwards that her dream of Olympic success had kept her going through the trials and tribulations of a career plagued by near misses, bad luck, and injury. She was just beaten into second place in the 1500 meters at the 1995 World Championships and was fourth at the 1996 Atlanta Olympics. Injury destroyed her chances for the 1500 meters in the 1997 World Championship. Many were beginning to doubt if she would ever win gold after she came third in the 800 meters in the Sydney Olympics in 2000 and second in the same event in the 2003 World Championships. "I could have given up. But I felt in my heart one day it might happen," she said. Holmes believes that the fluctuations in her success have made her the athlete she has become, strengthening her resolve to fulfill her dream.

There is a great deal of learning in Holmes' story for us all, particularly how her vision sustained her through difficult times, helping to keep the faith and maintaining her self-belief. Her story also highlights how sport can play a central part in our lives. It is a sphere of activity that allows us to express our character and to test ourselves, emotionally and physically. We need to master technical skills, cooperate with others, and summon from deep within emotional reserves of will and determination. These demands combine to make the field of sport an area that provides breadth of challenge and learning opportunities across many dimensions.

These are some clues about why I am encouraging you to visit the sports club and meet people for whom sport has played an important part in their lives and still does.

Most of us intuitively believe involvement in sport is a good thing. There have been debates whether we should put emphasis on competition in sports at school. Frankly I do believe we should maintain a competitive element. Competition can be against standards as well as competitors, and only by striving to do better do we increase our capacities. I agree that we need to take care in the way we nurture the competitive spirit in children, helping them to maintain their own and others' dignity in the face of victory and defeat. Helping children to recognize that the sense of frustration, disappointment, and even anger in defeat are great learning opportunities. After all, it isn't making mistakes that is so important but how we respond when they occur.

We have all heard the stories of great sporting achievement and the parallels that are drawn by commentators with greatness in other fields of human endeavor. Some of you may have heard successful athletes speak at conferences organized by companies or professional associations, and been inspired. I was privileged a few years ago to invite an Olympic champion to speak to colleagues about his unexpected success. I was deeply moved as he described openly the challenges he faced and the drama of the event. When he showed the film of his team winning gold, there were tears in my eyes. Afterwards, I felt honored to hold his gold medal. I felt inspired, but I doubt whether it changed the way I approached my job. What is unexpected about the stories you will hear as we visit the sports club is the way people have drawn powerful lessons from either participating in sport or watching others achieve.

Andy, vice president of a global software company, makes very specific linkages between his involvement in sport and his role leading business development in the financial services sector. He had a distinguished rugby career, playing for Welsh Schools and English Students. He was a Cambridge blue, and played as a

23-year-old for England B against Spain and Italy. Blessed with the gift of good hand–eye coordination, he nurtured this attribute, focusing predominately on the physical side of his game. Here he tells us how rugby has influenced his own development:

> Sport has been a significant part of my life and I draw many parallels between sport and business/professional life. Rugby was a major influence in my formative years. It taught me the basics of how teamwork can consistently overcome individual excellence, the fundamental importance of leadership, the importance of good coaching, the importance of good preparation, the need to step out of your comfort zone if you want to explore how good you can really be, and how personal relationships transcend geographic and time barriers.
>
> I paid no attention to mental preparation. In fact wasn't even aware of the need to do that. As I played at increasingly higher levels, I noticed that at times my confidence levels fluctuated and the lower they were, the more my performance suffered. Had I focused more on preparing mentally for big matches, I believe I would have progressed to even higher levels in international rugby. When I later worked with an executive coach I drew on these earlier experiences in developing an approach to my professional life, making time and space for mental preparation.
>
> This has raised my own awareness of my strengths and weaknesses and above all has helped me maintain self-belief in the face of major challenges. These changes I am sure have significantly contributed to my promotion to the UK board of our company.

Andy is a very keen sportsmen and golf has now replaced rugby as his greatest sporting interest, certainly as a player. He has drawn these specific lessons from the way he has worked on his golf game:

Golf has been an important influence from a different perspective. Golf, unlike rugby, is a solitary game where you compete against yourself all the time. Golf has taught me the discipline of being able to 'fall into the zone' (during a four-hour round of golf, the really important times are the 30-second zones of concentration when you are hitting the ball). It is vital that you are able to relax outside of the zone but switch into a highly concentrated state when required. Business life is exactly the same. Playing golf has also reinforced the importance of mental preparation, setting goals, and achieving milestones.

It is worth picking up on the point Andy makes about milestones. He started taking golf seriously about three years ago when his handicap was 13. He set himself the goal of reducing his handicap to 6. To get there, he set milestones. First the easy wins: improving your grip, stance, and swing can deliver significant benefits relatively quickly. The next goal is to get into what they call in golf Category 1, which is reaching a handicap of six or less. Reducing your handicap below six represents an exponentially increasing degree of difficulty, and is more about mental preparation, for example, thinking about the impact of the next shot and the one after that when hitting the ball in certain areas of the course.

Andy's goal is now to get to scratch, that is, a handicap of zero, and he has started to play at that level. His challenge now is to do that consistently. Andy believes that it is essential for him to make major commitments in time and emotional energy when pursuing ever-challenging goals, whether they are career or hobbies. He points out that you do need to be aware of what that commitment entails, and be willing to make the necessary sacrifices in other parts of your life before deciding on your professional and life goals. He finishes by summarizing the impact that sport has had on his business and personal life:

Sport has engendered in me the burning desire to

succeed and to be "the best I can possibly be." Sport, at the highest level, is all about winning, optimizing your ability and performance and finding ways to overcome competition—the very best sportsmen in the world achieve all of this with a smile on their face which often belies the intensity and hard work that has taken them to where they are. Business for me has many parallels.

The next sports enthusiast we meet is Lesley, who is CEO of a health care business. She has an interesting tale to tell about how she successfully applied training techniques to her business that had previously helped her succeed as an international rower. This is her story:

> As a student I rowed internationally and trained for around five hours every day. As well as the obvious physical challenge, I also learnt a lot about visualization techniques and something our coach referred to as "wave training."
>
> At university, I wasn't really big enough for rowing until they introduced the "lightweight" class and then I got into the Oxford lightweight fours. The GB team had just been selected for the world championships and as London-centric people had more visibility, the GB team was full of them. We believed we were as good if not better and we issued a challenge. If Oxford could beat the current GB team, we would represent Britain in the championships.
>
> I was very fortunate to spend nine months working with a great coach from whom I learnt a great deal. He was very innovative. He encouraged us to embrace doubts about our success. For example, when we were about to start a race and niggling doubts began to surface in our minds, he discouraged us from pushing the thought away. Instead, he told us to recall an occasion when we had started really well, to get in touch with how

it had felt at that time, then approach the task facing us. As we followed his advice, our confidence soared and we performed well. I have since used this technique on many occasions when dealing with problems in business that I initially doubted I could resolve.

The "wave training" approach was very sophisticated and has had an enduring effect on me as a business leader. It required us to train our bodies to peak at regular fortnightly intervals, allowing down time in-between. I learnt that you can keep your body at peak for limited periods and increase your capacity by ensuring that subsequent fortnightly peaks got progressively higher, even though there was quite a gap between the peaks and dips. So we might peak with a time of 1 minute 45 seconds for 500 metres then do 1 minute 55 seconds for the same distance when we dipped. The good news is that on the appointed day, we beat the GB team and went onto represent our country at the world championships.

Lesley has since learnt to apply this approach in business by allowing the organization she leads to "pace change." She calls it "pacing the organization."

She takes up the story:

I ran a business operating in a niche market. We were focused on back office, supply, production, and customer management. Overnight the other new competitors came back into the market. We now needed to take a different approach increasing our focus on sales and marketing.

Our market place was very traditional and the culture across the sector very conservative. Rather than drive change from the top, I had to pace the organization, legitimizing the need for change through a combination of strategic direction and bottom-up process change. I put a lot of effort into building a coalition behind me to support new initiatives.

I remember very well a dinner with my team. I asked them what signals they were picking up and what the gossip was. It emerged that there were serious concerns in the market about the performance of a competitor's product. My natural reaction was to drive through change to exploit the competitor's weakness. Yet the consensus around the table was "do nothing." I decided not to challenge this view in public. Instead I decided to work through the marketing director, rather than lead the change from the front. He became a convert to the need for change and then a champion. We subsequently decided to reposition our product, emphasizing its competitive advantages. We were so successful that our competitors closed the plant producing the product within six months! If I had tried to drive the change from the top, it would have taken much longer. They were facing change on so many fronts that taking on another one would just have slowed them down. Allowing them to start slowly and pick up the pace when they were ready delivered results. Over a period of three years the business was transformed from production to marketing driven. Profitability rose by 20 percent and market share increased by 25 percent.

So by drawing on her realization that you cannot perform at peak levels all the time, Lesley allowed her managers to take the initiative when they were ready. By taking this approach, she achieved a great deal more than if she had tried to dictate the pace from the outset.

Helena, who is a partner in a public relations firm, tells us how she gained some insights about the career path she has followed by reflecting on her interest in horse riding. She explains:

I took up riding because I was afraid of horses and forced

myself to work with them. I now do dressage, which is like ballet on horseback. You have to work with horses as partners, be aware of their moods and learn how to give instruction. When you do dressage you can't think of anything else. The insight I gained from this is realizing that my approach to equestrian sports mirrors my approach to my career, which must reflect an important emotional driver. I've always had jobs that take me right out of my comfort zone, moving from research to advertising to brand strategy to finance and corporate communications. It is helpful to be aware of this, as it provides valuable clues to where I get my energy from, and of course the type of work I should seek and of course avoid.

As well as helping you prepare for a business career, involvement in sport can also help you put the challenges you face at work into perspective. Jim, who is head of commercial development for a retail bank, explains:

I was involved in competitive sport long before I had a career, and enjoyed some success in athletics, orienteering, long-distance walking, and sailing. As a 15-year-old schoolboy I was part of a team of six boys that broke an endurance record set by marines, running 80 miles in 24 hours. Through my involvement in sport, I learnt so much about coaching, getting the most out of teams, striving for stretch goals, being competitive and organized. All of this really laid the foundations for my management career. I learned more about training teams and discipline in sport than any time behind a desk.

Sailing has stretched my capabilities across a wide spectrum, and has provided challenges which are as much about character as about seamanship. When you are at sea, you can't transfer staff in and out, you've got what you've got and have to make the best of it. The situations I have found myself in at sea have tested my judgment in a way that doesn't happen often in an office environment. For example, I can recall bringing a boat back to England from Portugal. In the middle of the night, there was a gale blowing. We were 200 miles from land and I could hear a clanking sound below. I feared the worst! The rudder! What should I do? If I wakened the crew, I would have created panic. I kept my cool under the pressure of responsibility. I went through the boat and checked it all out thoroughly. Imagine my relief when I discovered it was a gas bottle that had come free of its fastening and was banging against the side. Faced with that kind of pressure, it puts the challenge of preparing a sales plan into perspective and consequently reduces the associated stress.

Playing sports can help develop specific skills that can be applied in business. Markus, a communications manager in a global energy firm, believes his experience of playing volleyball helped develop his ability to be flexible in decision making and adaptable in approach to team working. Both characteristics are essential for effective working in his managing communications in a very complex and dynamic organization. In his current role, he needs to be constantly adapting to change and collaborating with colleagues across the organization. He brings out the importance of these characteristics in his description of the sport:

I was a very keen volleyball player. I tried soccer but preferred a non-contact sport. In volleyball, success is based on generalists. Everyone plays in every position at some point in the game and everyone has to be able to play the full range of shots. The secret is in selecting the right individual with the right qualities in specific situations as the game progresses. In work, team sports are often used in leadership models. A lot of men use the metaphors of the captain and team players who follow.

Volleyball can't be played that way: because of the rotation and need to be adaptable, leadership roles must rotate. This is more akin to life in a large, complex, modern corporation. I believe playing volleyball is an excellent preparation for that.

By studying the approach of a great England cricket captain and applying the lessons to his own game, Neill, a partner in a financial services firm, developed insights about the role he could play in bringing out the best in others. He found that captaining a cricket eleven of diverse individuals helped him understand how different motivational techniques are required with different people.

Some captains lead by example. Some by creating an environment in which team members can flourish. You don't have to be the best player in the team to be the best captain! I remember reading *The Art of Captaincy* by Mike Brearley, the former England cricket captain. If ever there was a sports book with wider relevance to the business world, this is it. It was from reading this book that I developed a simple philosophy that motivation of team members is complex but can often be reduced to "carrot and stick." Some people need a carrot and others need a stick, while some characters need a bit of both! It also helped me realize that personally I fall into the carrot category. I also realized that many leaders in organizations that I have previously worked for would have been more effective if they had recognized what motivated the people who worked for them.

Jeremy, commercial director of a publishing group, draws parallels between the inevitable fluctuations in sporting performance and those in business. He argues that we must pay attention to them if we are to get the best out of people.

Even great sports teams don't win every game. Great soccer players don't score in every game; great baseball players don't hit a home run in every innings. All great teams and players suffer slumps from time to time. It is essential to bear this in mind when evaluating business performance. Short-term performance of individuals and businesses will often be volatile, but what matters is what happens over the medium to long term. I play tennis and golf. Some days I play well, other days not, but my average game is quite good. When you have achieved a degree of competence, you should be able to do that consistently. That's logical, yet it doesn't always happen, and it is much more pronounced at professional level. Look at Tiger Woods's results in the pairs in the 2004 Ryder Cup. Even Michael Schumacher doesn't win every race. The same applies in business. For example, we expect salesmen to deliver results consistently, yet I've found that if they hit a slump and have been good performers in the past, they will do a good job in the future, and it has proved to be right. When that's the case I stuck with them, and have been invariably proved right.

Jeff, sales and marketing director for a consumer goods company, is a great sports enthusiast. His discovery was gained as a result of a hobby he took up because of his interest in football.

My interest in sport led me to develop a sport prediction game. It prompted my first foray into the Internet, where I play the game with a group of friends, business colleagues, and customers. The game is based on each player making predictions about the results of soccer matches in the English Premier League. The games have provided me with a good method of keeping in touch with important clients without the need for a business reason, and it has helped with customer relations management. Interest in the game has spread, and there are now over 1000 people playing it. I communicate directly with about 50 people on a regular basis. Setting up and running the games also helped me understand the logistics and economics of the Internet, including the different business models you can use. It showed me how the Internet market was evolving. This allowed me to develop my creativity in an area I enjoy. It helped me acquire skills and knowledge that stood me in good stead when I established an Internet exchange linking my own company, competitors, and suppliers, to help us better trade the component parts that make up the products we supply to customers.

Most of the people you have met here so far have told you stories about how they have learnt from playing or watching sport. Learning how to master the techniques required and coping with the successes and disappointments have clearly been very influential in the lives and careers of these people.

Swag, financial director of a healthcare company, now takes us to a place popularly known by the fans of the world-famous English football team that plays there as the "theater of dreams." That place is Old Trafford and the team is Manchester United, which Swag, who was born and brought up in Manchester, has supported since he was a boy. Swag takes us there as a spectator and speaks to us about his admiration, not for the players but of their manager Sir Alex Ferguson.

I have been particularly influenced as a businessman in two ways by Sir Alex Ferguson's approach.

Firstly the way he tailors his management of players according to that particular individual's requirements. For example, he has always appeared to treat Ryan Giggs as an adult. He broke through into the first team when he was very young. An outstanding talent, he could easily have been distracted, yet while under Ferguson's management he has always conducted himself well and

61

has been a credit to his profession; a great role model to youngsters. Giggs has proved himself to be a very loyal servant to the club, and Ferguson's ability is evident in his handling of another world-class player, Dutch striker Ruud van Nistelrooy. When his transfer from PSV Eindhoven of Holland fell through, a few years ago, due to injury, Ferguson could have lost interest and turned his attentions elsewhere. Instead he stayed in touch, showed faith and confidence in the player, building a relationship that enabled him to sign the Dutch star, in face of competition on his return to fitness and form.

Secondly, the way he is able to motivate his players, to raise their games, turning around what looks like a lost cause and securing victory. It is significant that Manchester United win many important games by scoring goals late in the game, often in extra time. The outstanding example of this was in the final of the European Champions League Final in 1999 when they defeated Bayern Munich of Germany 2–1 at the Nou Camp stadium in Barcelona. United had been outplayed by Bayern and were still one goal down in the dying minutes. Late in the game Ferguson had sent on Sheringham and Solskjaer as substitutes As they took the field, rather than "Get us back into this game" he said: "We've lost the first game 1–0, we now need to go out and win the second game by at least two goals." Sheringham scored a goal a minute into extra time, leveling the score, and Solskjaer scored the winner a minute later as United won 2–1 and took the Champions League title.

The Norwegian Solskjaer was another great example of someone who was very loyal to Ferguson. In the previous season, the club had considered transferring him. He had not been the first choice striker and with the impending arrival of van Nistelrooy, his future was in question. He had been disappointed by the club's apparent willingness to sell him and asked to stay and fight for his place. Ferguson supported him and on that spring evening in Barcelona, Solskjaer proved his detractors wrong and repaid the faith Ferguson had kept in him.

These are great examples of people management. Ferguson like everyone makes mistakes, but he gets more right than he gets wrong, and his record speaks for itself.

Swag highlights Sir Alex Ferguson's skills as a tactician and motivator. These are essential qualities of a successful people manager. It is his ability to continually nurture and replenish a pool of talented players that has sustained the outstanding success of Manchester United under his influence since the early 1990s. This track record has made United the envy of many football clubs and indeed business organizations, as they have become more conscious of the need to manage talent.

Ed Michaels, Helen Handfield-Jones, and Beth Axelrod, of the management consulting firm McKinsey, brought the importance of talent to prominence. In 2001 they published a report on *The War for Talent*. Since then many major business corporations have embarked on strategies for accelerating the development of their high-potential employees. In his book on *Managing Talent* Roger Cartwright has featured Manchester United and Sir Alex Ferguson as an example of best practice. A vigorous youth development scheme has consistently yielded a harvest of outstanding home-grown players, demonstrating maturity beyond their years. They have been blended imaginatively with a diverse collection of foreign players. Players from many countries have contributed to United's success, including Argentina, Denmark, France, Holland, Norway, Portugal, and Uruguay. In addition to nurturing players, Ferguson has been decisive in letting players go when they are no longer making the contribution required, whether they are nearing the end of their career or are no longer compatible with their team mates and the system of playing.

Here are some key learning points of Manchester United's success. Talent is not confined to one ethnic group or nation. Cultural norms may help or hinder the opportunities for individuals to display talent, so United's international following and reputation helped foster amongst supporters a willingness to welcome foreign players. Multinational teams can work success-fully together. Finally, stereotyping can lead to talent being under-utilized. At the start of the 1995/96 season a television pundit asserted, "You'll never win anything with kids." At the end of the season Manchester United had won the 1995/96 Premiership title again, and this time with five players under the age of 21. As Cartwright concludes, "Ferguson's ability to reach and motivate across cultural, national and language barriers is the reason he is considered one of the all-time great managers in what is a truly international game."

I am sure you will agree that this visit to the sports club has yielded a great deal of insights about building loyalty motivation, mental preparation, adaptability, pacing change, fluctuations in performance, and managing talent.

5
ART GALLERY

THE NEXT PLACE I am taking you to is the art gallery. We will attend a presentation by an expert in creativity, then we will meet a couple of artists. One works in business full time and paints for a hobby. The other paints full time and works mostly with organizations. We will complete our visit after you have had an opportunity to participate in a creative workshop.

Visual art is probably the most familiar of the creative techniques used in organizations. People talk a lot about the "vision" for their business or department. Visual images are often referred to by questions such as "So what does the future look like for the company?" Even though technology enables us to make use of high-impact visual images, most visions are communicated in words, often in bullet-point form.

Right and left brain

We make our way into the lecture theater. It is lunchtime and the theater is half full, which is more than I expected. The audience looks like a mixture of students, tourists and office workers on their breaks. The speaker is a professor from an American university. He is very engaging and the energy levels in the room lift as he begins to talk.

He begins by asking the audience whether any of us have ever attended a training course where the facilitator has asked us to draw a picture of ourselves as a leader, or perhaps describing our company's relationships with customers. About a quarter of the audience raise their hands. He suggests that the trainer may then have encouraged us and fellow participants to explore the meaning of the image we created and draw out learnings. Visual images are used in this way because they engage what is commonly referred to as the right brain. The idea that the human brain has two very different ways of thinking developed from research in the late 1960s by an American psychologist, Roger Sperry, and that will be the subject of the talk we are attending.

We are told that Sperry discovered that the two different sides of the brain (hemispheres) control two different ways of thinking, and each of us prefers one way to the other. The right brain is visual and processes information in an intuitive and simultaneous way, looking first at the whole or "big picture" then the details. In contrast the left brain is verbal, and processes information in an analytical and sequential way, looking first at the pieces then putting them together to get the whole picture. Sperry was awarded a Nobel Prize for his work in 1981.

We are then shown the chart on page 71, which summarizes how the right and left brain focus their attention.

When you look at this comparison you start to get some clues about why a trainer or facilitator wants you to engage your right brain on a workshop, particularly at the beginning. It's not that right-brain is better than left-brain thinking; they are simply two different ways of thinking. It is important to be aware that there are these different ways of thinking, to know what your natural preference is, and to be open to new approaches that are different from your natural inclination. That in itself is a source of learning. The reason why training/learning facilitators encourage workshop participants to take a right-brain approach is because it is considered to be more creative. This is often particularly helpful at the beginning of a workshop, or when participants are about to be presented with something new.

An important element of learning is about gaining new knowledge and skills. If you look down the right-brain column it should be clear why these characteristics are helpful in a learning situation, particularly early in a program. If you tend to be intuitive, following "gut feel," you see the whole first then the details, work on several ideas at the same time, and like to know why you are doing something or why rules exist. You will also be more likely to consider new things, see how they fit together and why they are important. This will really help you get started with your learning, and it is why these approaches are encouraged at the start of learning events. When these characteristics are combined with the left-brain attributes of analysis—planning and organization—you have the capability to effectively deepen understanding by applying your learning. So the more right-brain your thinking is, the more naturally curious you are likely to be, and the more willing to explore new places and experiences. Right-brain thinking with its emphasis on patterns and the big picture also helps with problem solving.

More recent research has shown that as far as the brain is concerned things aren't quite as polarized. Experiments have shown that both sides of the brain are active when dealing with areas that were presumed to be processed exclusively by one side or the other in the original research. So when it comes to language, the left side deals with grammar and word production while the right side deals with aspects such as intonation and emphasis. Similarly the right brain is active when looking at pictures and working with a general sense of space, while the left brain is active when thinking about particular objects. But the tendencies described in the chart shown on page 71 still hold true.

How the right and left brain focus their attention

Left brain	Right brain
Verbal, focus on words, symbols, numbers	Visual, focus on images and patterns
Analytical, led by logic	Intuitive, following "gut feel"
Works through one idea at a time, step by step	Works on several ideas at the same time
Makes logical deductions from information	Makes lateral connections from information
Makes lists and plans	Free association
Work up to the whole step by step, focusing on details	Sees the whole first then the details
Tends to follow rules without questioning them	Likes to know why we are doing something or why rules exist
Good at keeping track of time	No sense of time
Plans ahead	Trouble prioritizing, so often late, impulsive
Likely to read instruction manual before using a new piece of equipment	Unlikely to read instruction manual before using a new piece of equipment
Listen to what is said	Listen to how something is said
Likely to believe you're not creative, need to be willing to try and take risks to develop your potential	Likely to think you're naturally creative, but need to apply yourself to develop your potential

You may be wondering what your own predisposition is, and having read these past few paragraphs you will certainly have a few clues. Running through the chart on page 71 should help you identify where your natural preferences are. If you are keen to check it out more thoroughly, keying "right and left brain thinking" into a search engine will point to several sites offering questionnaires to help you clarify your preference. You are likely to have a distinct preference for one orientation over the other.

Formal education traditionally favors left-brain modes of thinking. Have you ever noticed that it doesn't always follow that all those who do best at school become the most successful? That might have something to do with the fact that studying for many academic subjects focuses on logical thinking, analysis, and accuracy. While these are important, people who tend to be more "right brained" are more likely to focus on feeling, making connections, creativity, and relationships. In an increasingly complex and unpredictable world, to be successful you need a good combination of both attributes. At school in the early years at least, children can win prizes with strengths primarily in left-brain thinking.

We are coming towards the end of the talk, and the speaker brings it elegantly to a conclusion by quoting Albert Einstein very powerfully articulating the case for right-brain thinking:

I am enough of an artist to draw freely upon my imagination. Imagination is more important than knowledge. Knowledge is limited. Imagination encircles the world.

We leave the lecture theater and now have a great opportunity to immediately put into practice what we have been hearing about. We are in an art gallery after all, and where better to engage in right-brain thinking? I decide we also need some material sustenance, and lead us into the café where we meet Markus. You will recall he works in communication with a large energy company. We sit down to have coffee in the atrium café. It has large windows looking out over the river and there is light coming down from the roof. The aroma of our coffee reaches me well before Markus brings it to our table. We talk about the subject of the lecture we have just attended, and speculate whether our preferences are for left or right brain thinking. Markus asks me if companies in financial services encourage art in the working environment. I tell him that many companies sponsor exhibitions and most have paintings. It has become quite fashionable to have expensive art in the reception areas of headquarters.

One company where the chairman is an enthusiastic art lover and has a policy of investing in art is Hiscox plc. This specialist insurer that generates most of its revenue from insurance premiums for valuable horses, fine art, and insuring celebrities from kidnap. Robert Hiscox is the chairman. Annual sales are approximately £600 million and it employs over 300 people. Hiscox developed an interest in fine art from an early age, and acknowledges that it has influenced many aspects of his business life directly and indirectly. As a boy he was always interested in antiques, persuading his father to buy items including paintings. He will tell you that he finds it very uplifting looking at pictures. Initially a major driver for him was how to make money to buy art. When he started working at Lloyd's as an insurance underwriter, he got interested in risks involving paintings and built a "book" of art insurance business. At the time he was the only person specializing in that field. He then created a new insurance product, separating art from household policies.

Robert Hiscox's love of art has also influenced his approach to business investment. He admits that he doesn't like buying shares in other companies, so he uses profits to buy paintings. He suggests that using this channel for profits has prevented the company from making acquisitions, particularly at times of consolidation in the insurance industry, that it could have subsequently regretted.

You may be wondering what impact, if any, the many paintings hanging on the Hiscox office have on the staff and the culture. Robert Hiscox believes that they are very popular in the firm, and paintings have become conversation pieces. The paintings are moved around not just in the London office but also to the company's international locations. They are used as a reward, and if you reach a particular business target you can have the painting of your choice in your area. His conviction is that "beautiful art has a civilizing effect on people." That's important to him because he tells us that at Hiscox they are trying to behave in a more civilized way towards colleagues and clients.

Hiscox plc pays attention to all aspects of the environment. Several years ago the company had to move into temporary accommodation as a result of bomb damage to its offices. Robert Hiscox himself and his colleagues really hated going there, but they didn't know why. They hired a feng shui consultant who applied the Chinese art of placement to their office. When they implemented the consultants' recommendations on office layout and furnishings, it worked. Here was evidence of how one's physical environment can affect staff morale.

The chairman's belief that the art has a positive effect on the company's culture is supported by Hiscox's high ranking in the 2004 *Sunday Times 100 Best Companies to Work For* In this survey 82 percent of Hiscox staff stated they believe that they can make a difference in the firm, and a similar number are excited about where the firm is going. The paintings were specifically mentioned by employees. Here are a couple of examples:

> I believe this is one of the best places to work because of the art and exhibitions.

> I have been able to get involved in the art project, which involves a new exhibition each month in the Art Cafe. It's great to see a company that is happy to allow employees to pursue other areas and support it.

So it seems that the company's imaginative engagement with art in the office environment is making a difference.

The story about Hiscox shows us what kind of impact hanging paintings on the office walls can have. It is really encouraging. It would also be interesting to hear about the impact that painting has on business people who take it up themselves as a hobby.

Markus tells us that he paints and has learnt a lot about himself from it. The materials he has chosen to paint with have probably provided more learning than the subject of his paintings. A few years ago he was on holiday with his wife and family in Denmark. They were staying at a cottage by the sea, but the weather was bad and stuck indoors, he was bored. To amuse himself he borrowed his wife's watercolors. This didn't work for him, as he recalls:

> The paints were too soft. You have to let them dry and then go over, shading a little here and there. That is not for me. I like the energy of expressing myself spontaneously in colour, and acrylic was much better for that, allowing me to make bold brush strokes. As a result, I learn that I am a process person, a phase person. Painting allows me to go through phases. I do things, let things happen, identify patterns then decide how to respond. There is an initial phase, then I let it go, let the energies flow and allow something to surface. This is the way I work in organizations.

It would be interesting to hear more about the use of art in business. There are artists who work with businesses to involve people in making change happen in their organisations. As we learnt at the lecture we attended, working with visual images engages the right brain. It stimulates creativity and helps people see the whole or the "big picture" and make connections. These attributes are essential when you are trying to bring about changes that affect many people across a company.

Artist Julian Burton's radical reworking of the old adage "a picture speaks a thousand words" is transforming the way his clients clarify and communicate their business challenges. He has worked with several well-known companies in banking, insurance, energy, telecommunications, and health care.

What happens when you work with an artist in this way? Julian helps people within organizations to translate their difficult and complex challenges into a large colorful picture.

Julian facilitates conversations between key groups of people whose commitment is required to meet these business challenges. He then translates important themes, issues, and insights that people have into pictures for everyone involved to see and reflect on as the discussions continue. The whole team can see what they and everyone else has said. Seeing what you are talking about translated into a tangible, visible form really focuses attention on important issues. It helps to give everybody an immediate grasp of the big picture in a way that is unavailable in words alone. The process of working with an artist in this way creates an opportunity for people to openly share their points of view and concerns. It pulls together different perspectives to build up a big picture which is a shared vision that everyone can agree to work towards. This approach enriches the work of the group and enhances its ability to focus on and create shared understanding and commitment.

Julian uses powerful and graphic imagery to represent the challenges and opportunities that organizations face. He often asks people to come up with a metaphor that represents their situation. So it could be a boat representing a restructured organization sailing in a river between the twin hazards of the whirlpool and waterfall. If they take the wrong course they could spin out of control in the whirlpool, or risk being swept over the waterfall if they try to stay still. In another organization we have leaders spinning plates, because there are so many priorities that there are no priorities!

Julian builds up the picture initially by drawing the images that are suggested to him by what people are saying. At the beginning there is not a lot of clarity, but as he starts to make the picture, things get clearer and more tangible. He then presents his draft big picture to the senior group, and when they agree it, he goes off and paints it in watercolors. One reaction to his work is that it does cause unease at times. In his experience, where there is anxiety and discomfort, that's a sign that there's something important that needs attention.

Once senior leaders have agreed the big picture they then take responsibility for facilitating people through a dialog about the pictures. It provides an opportunity for people to tell their own story and hear others'. When the leaders and their staff are looking at a big colorful object together, it becomes a common point of reference. They are not facing each other and it is less confrontational. The way people interpret the pictures reflects their current concerns. People talk about what is important to them.

People typically respond very well when their bosses facilitate a dialog with them and colleagues about a big picture. Here a senior manager in an insurance company describes how she experienced the process:

> I facilitated six of our people in London through a conversation about the big picture that we have produced for our division. Their response was very positive. They told us it was great to know we had a vision, great to experience leadership, and great to be consulted. The process is so powerful in its simplicity. What was unexpected was the way people reacted. When they came into the room, they sat down at the table. They were expecting the usual: to be talked at, perhaps a bullet-point PowerPoint presentation. So they sat down at the table. We had to get them to move away to look at the picture. When they looked at it, they realized they were in pain and knew they had to go on a journey. By looking and talking about the picture, they came away more positive.
>
> Working with this picture enabled me to walk six people through the story, allowed them to articulate what the vision meant to them. They realized they had more pain to go through, but when they were through it they would be in a better place. They also challenged

me and were very clear about their expectations. They told me I had better deliver my part of the bargain, and they then told me how they could support realization of this vision. A colleague observing commented on how the language had changed. At the beginning, they were talking about them and us. As we progressed we were only talking about "us."

It's a bit ironic that we have spent a lot of time talking about images here, so before we move on I want to give you an opportunity to experience what it is like to engage with a picture that an artist has created which relates to your experience of work.

Opposite is an excerpt from a big picture that Julian Burton created some time ago. It is *The horrific diary* and I imagine is an idea that you can relate to. Take some time to look at that image on your own. Pause and quietly reflect on what it means to you. You may want to do this next part with some colleagues.

Ask yourself these questions:

- What do you see in this picture?

- What does it mean to you?

- How would you change the picture to make it more meaningful and relevant to you?

- Would you add anything or take away something?

- How does this picture relate to your experience?

- Does it prompt you to do anything? What?

- Does it prompt you to ask others to do something? Who? What?

The horrific diary – Julian Burton

- Finally, having seen this image, are you noticing anything different and are you now thinking and feeling differently about your situation?

What will you do now?

6
THEATER

OUR NEXT STOP is the theater. Why are we going there? You have been there before: perhaps at school where you performed in school plays, or you might have helped with the lighting and props when your classmates trod the boards. Then there were the pantomimes you enjoyed with parents and often grandparents when you were small. Most of us have visited the theater at some time in our lives: perhaps the occasional visit to a show or musical in London, or to a local production. So you may agree that you will probably enjoy a visit to the theater. It will be entertaining if I chose something you like, but you may doubt whether you are really going to learn much that you can use at work, or anywhere else for that matter.

The answer will become clear as we proceed with our visit. In the meantime, I'll let the greatest playwright of all time, William Shakespeare, give you a clue with this quote from *As You Like It*:

All the world's a stage.
And all the men and women merely players.
They have their exits and their entrances,
And one man in his time plays many parts.
(*As You Like It*, Act 2, Sc 8, 139–43)

On arrival at the theater our friend Adrian meets us. He is a very good actor and performs as a hobby. When he was at college he acted in many plays, winning awards and performing at the Edinburgh Festival. When he is not acting he is a very successful senior executive in a large international bank. He will be soon be performing on stage, and tells us about his love of acting and what it gives him. He apologizes but he has to rush and get ready.

We make our way into the stalls. On our way in we buy a program of the evening's production. It seems quite unusual and reads as shown on the opposite page.

Discovery Theater

Evening Program

✩✩✩

The Fish from the Sea The Tonbridge Players
The Maltese Falcon The Tonbridge Players

✩✩✩

Interval

✩✩✩

Workshop on *Henry V* by William Shakespeare

✩✩✩

Interval

✩✩✩

Poetry workshop

Normally when you come to theater you see one play. This program has three plays and a poetry reading. But this is a program I've had specially put together for us. So Adrian's Tonbridge Players will perform selected excerpts from their productions.

What's this workshop on *Henry V*? And Shakespeare? You may not have enjoyed Shakespeare at school, just memorizing your classmates' notes to scrape through exams. And how relevant is all that stuff nowadays? Relax. The workshop you will experience is based on the work of Richard Olivier and the Olivier Mythodrama Associates They are a group of people who run workshops about Shakespeare plays for people working in organizations. They present and perform parts of the plays that will interest you. There is usually an opportunity to join in and do a a bit of acting for us all. You'll enjoy it. Trust me. And finally, you'll be pleasantly surprised and inspired.

The interval is a great time to have a drink and chat about what we've seen. It will be even better tonight because I've arranged for some of those performing to come and talk to us, as well as the people taking part in the workshop.

Thinking on your feet

The lights go down and the Tonbridge Players take to the stage. We can see our friend Adrian. *The Fish from the Sea* is set in the nineteenth century. Adrian is with a group of men, unloading a catch of fish from their boat. We next see a woman seated on a chair in front of a fire, by a table, apparently writing a letter. We know from Adrian that this is the sister of the character he plays. Adrian walks through the door, having changed out of his fisherman's clothes, and asks his sister who she is writing to. When she answers that she is writing to their cousin, his mood changes abruptly. He berates her and quickly loses his temper.

The scene is intended to be tense, yet despite excellent acting by our friend that is not the mood in the theater. It is quite the opposite. There is an undercurrent of laughter in the audience, and the actors begin to look puzzled. The woman playing the sister looks across at Adrian and notices something, then raises her eyes to meet his. He fears the worst. You can imagine him thinking, "Oh, no. When I did that quick change … My God. Have I left my flies undone?" He has the presence of mind to move behind the table and looks down. The horror on his face says it all. He *has* left his flies undone. He reaches down and with one deft movement zips them shut. The impending decline into farce of this serious dramatic performance was halted.

The acting continues for another 20 minutes.

The lights go down and we can hear movement in the darkness as the stage is prepared for an excerpt of the Tonbridge Players' production of *The Maltese Falcon*. The curtain raises and we are looking at a scene in a room in an apartment. Our friend Adrian again appears on stage. He is working hard tonight. He is playing Sam Spade, private eye, the character played by Humphrey Bogart in the 1941 film version. He engages in a very lively and animated conversation. The characters are talking quickly and loudly. Then in mid-sentence, silence. It's inexplicable. Both actors glance awkwardly at each other. There is a very uneasy silence, which pervades the whole theater. Now the audience knows something is wrong. It's one of those embarrassing situations which seem to last an age. But in reality, less than a minute has passed. Then Adrian jumps up and proclaims, "Well if they don't phone us, I'll call them." He picks up the phone and simulates making a call. The audience breathes a collective sigh of relief. It seems that the phone was supposed to ring in the middle of the conversation, but it didn't and the actors had no cue. As a result they lost momentum until Adrian recovered.

Discovering learning during the interval

At the interval, Adrian has finished for the night and we meet him in the bar for a drink. I say to him, 'You acted well tonight, but it was a bit fraught at times. How did you feel on those two occasions when things went awry?'

Adrian replied like this:

> Thank you, I love acting and it has taught me to think on my feet in public without panicking and covering mistakes on stage, like tonight. I spend a lot of time in my job doing presentations and things often go wrong. But you just have to get on with it and improvise like I did tonight. Acting has taught me to rehearse meticulously, almost word perfect. I always do that when I present, taking the full script with me. I can remember one occasion when I opened my notes and the first page was missing. I carried on unperturbed as I had thoroughly prepared, and when I eventually found the page I checked and found I had only missed out one word. I have learnt more from acting about presentation and thinking on my feet than anything else I have ever done.

Inspirational leadership

The bell goes, signalling the end of the interval, so we say our thanks and goodbyes to Adrian and make our way back to our seats ready for the next performance. As we do so, I sense you are about to challenge me with something like: "I know Shakespeare was a great writer and his plays are still performed around the world. But what has it got to do with our lives today?" I am initially tempted to argue that the themes of Shakespeare's plays are time-less and the insights offered to us about our lives and relationships are just as relevant today as they were in Elizabethan England. But I won't do that. Instead, to demonstrate that the words of the great bard touch our lives today and almost every day, I'll urge you to consider this:

> If you cannot understand my argument, and declare "It's Greek to me," you are quoting Shakespeare;
>
> If you claim to be more sinned against than sinning, you are quoting Shakespeare;
>
> If you recall your salad days, you are quoting Shakespeare;
>
> If you act more in sorrow than in anger, if your wish is father to the thought, if your property has vanished into thin air, you are quoting Shakespeare;
>
> If you have ever refused to budge an inch or suffered from green-eyed jealousy, if you have played fast and loose, if you have been tongue-tied, a tower of strength, hoodwinked or in a pickle, if you have knitted your brows, made a virtue of necessity, insisted on fair play, slept not one wink, stood on ceremony, danced atten-dance (on your lord and master), laughed yourself into stitches, had short shrift, cold comfort or too much of a good thing, if you have seen better days or lived in a fool's paradise – why, be that as it may, the more fool you, for it is a foregone conclusion that you are (as good luck would have it) quoting Shakespeare;

If you think it is early days and clear out bag and baggage, if you think it is high time and that is the long and the short of it, if you believe that the game is up and that truth will out even if it involves your own flesh and blood, if you lie low till the crack of doom because you suspect foul play, if you have your teeth set on edge (at one fell swoop) without rhyme or reason, then to give the devil his due – if the truth were known (for surely you have a tongue in your head) you are quoting Shakespeare;

Even if you bid me good riddance and send me packing, if you wish I were dead as a door-nail, if you think I am an eyesore, a laughing stock, the devil incarnate, a stony hearted villain, bloody minded or a blinking idiot, then – by Jove! O Lord! Tut, tut! for goodness sake! What the dickens! But no buts – it is all one to me, for you are quoting Shakespeare.

Bernard Levin

We settle down waiting for the lights to go down but nothing happens. Instead of actors appearing in costume, the stage is suddenly full of people, about 20 of them, sitting on chairs in a circle. In front of them is a man talking, and to his left is a flipchart. He is an actor, and seated in a circle around him are people from businesses and public-sector organizations who have come on this workshop based on Henry V, the inspirational leader

We hear that of all Shakespeare's plays, *Henry V* is the one from which we can learn most about inspiration. These lessons are to be found not only in the great speeches but woven into the fabric of incidents throughout the play. Richard Olivier has written a book called *Inspirational Leadership: Henry V and the Muse of Fire*, which describes these in detail. We will hear about a selection at today's workshop, which is intended to give people a taster of the experience.

We listen to an overview of the story, using language similar to that used in modern business:

Henry V unites a group of disparate people (his nobles) around a common goal (reclaiming the territory of France) and manages to overcome all difficulties in his path to achieve a near-miraculous victory against the odds (winning the battle of Agincourt).

We are invited us to see "… the King as an inspired leader, the nation as an organization, the nobles as a senior management team, France as a big project or territory there is reason to claim …."

You may still be wondering what you can learn from Shakespeare's *Henry V*. If we were to participate in the full workshop, we would hear speeches and presentations at each stage. We would also do some exercises that include role-playing. To help explain this, Richard Olivier and his colleagues use a diagram (see opposite) to map each of the key leadership challenges that Henry faces.

Most of these terms will be familiar, and the relevance to modern-day business should become apparent with a bit of imagination, but there are a few that need some explanation, particularly "The dark night of the soul" and "Turning the battlefield into a garden." Henry also has to decide to "Leave the pub" before he can become king, a challenge that many of us face from time to time. Let's begin to draw out the relevance of this story for modern times.

Henry's Journey

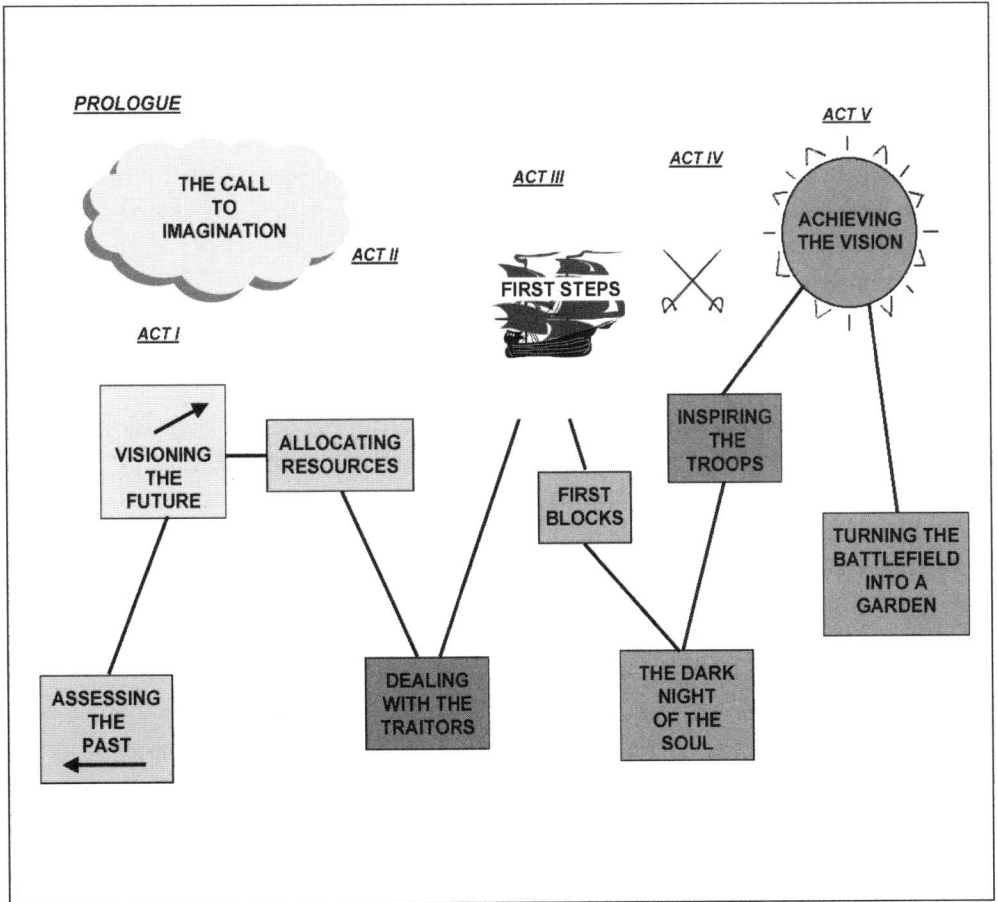

PROLOGUE

THE CALL
TO
IMAGINATION

ACT II

FIRST STEPS

ACT I

VISIONING
THE
FUTURE

ALLOCATING
RESOURCES

ACT III

FIRST
BLOCKS

ACT IV

ACT V

ACHIEVING
THE VISION

INSPIRING
THE
TROOPS

TURNING THE
BATTLEFIELD
INTO A
GARDEN

ASSESSING
THE
PAST

DEALING
WITH THE
TRAITORS

THE DARK
NIGHT
OF THE
SOUL

"Henry's Journey" map. © 2002 Olivier Mythodrama Associates.

Leaving the pub

Where better to start than the pub? Before becoming king, Henry, known then as Prince Hal, had led a riotous life and had been keeping the sort of company your parents wouldn't approve of. When he becomes king, after his father dies, he is faced with the question of how to make the transition from being one of the lads to becoming a respected monarch. Hence the question "How to leave the pub?" This a question commonly faced by people as they are promoted above their peers, especially when some of them have been close friends. It is a difficult one for many, as Richard points out: "A leader can never be just one of the lads." There has to be some distancing to enable the leader to maintain some degree of objectivity, and to be seen as having his or her own identity and not being too close to any particular group. Henry is confronted with this challenge when at his coronation, his old friend Falstaff shouts to him, calling him "my sweet boy." Henry deals with him by responding as follows:

> I know thee not, old man, fall to thy prayers …
> Presume not that I am the thing I was.

He banishes Falstaff not to come within ten miles of him, and in so doing puts a distance, literally in this case, between himself and his former drinking partners, to enable him to appropriately discharge the responsibilities of his office and be seen to do so.

Dark night of the soul

"What about this dark night of the soul? The French army of 40,000 soldiers outnumbers the English five to one. They have surrounded Henry and his men at the field of Agincourt. He declines an offer of truce from the French in return for surrendering and paying a huge fine. Both sides prepare for battle. Henry's dark night is the one before the battle, when he has to face up to his fears and responsibilities before he is ready to lead his troops to victory. He refuses a request from his nobles for a meeting, saying: "I and my bosom must debate awhile and then I would no other company." He then disguises himself and walks unrecognized amongst the soldiers, who are afraid and blaming him for their predicament. He spends time alone to unload some of the burden of his responsibilities, and then he is ready to re-engage with his nobles and get ready for the battle.

The relevance of Henry's dark night to modern business is that there comes a point in most major projects or initiatives when we ask ourselves if it is worth it. Can you achieve what you have set out to? Do you have the right people, and are you the right person to lead them? At times like this we have to put on a brave face for our people, but pay attention to what is going on for us, our own fears and anxieties. Henry spends time with his troops to understand their hopes and fears. This is essential if he is to motivate them later. He also needs to unload the burden of responsibilities he feels, if he is to be able to stand back and make decisions based on what is required rather than his own selfish needs at that point. By taking time to appreciate the emotions of his men and of himself, he is better placed to make the right decisions and lead them to victory.

He is next confronted by his nobles' concerns that they are heavily outnumbered. Henry is now ready to inspire them to battle, addressing them as his "band of brothers" and painting a vivid picture for them of what it will be like when the battle is over and they have returned home safely:

This day is called the Feast of Crispian.
He that outlives this day and comes safe home
Will stand a-tiptoe when this day is named
And rouse him at the name of Crispian.
He that shall see this day and live old age
Will yearly on the vigil feast his neighbours
And say, 'Tomorrow is Saint Crispian.'
Then will he strip his sleeve and show his scars
And say, 'These wounds I had on Crispin's day'
Old men forget; yet all shall be forgot,
But he'll remember with advantages,
What feats he did that day. Then shall our names,
Familiar in his mouth as household words...
Be in their flowing cups freshly remembered.

(Henry V, Act 4, Sc. 3)

Turning the battlefield into a garden

"What is the point of the garden? Simply put, in Act V of the play, Henry is encouraged to turn the battlefield into a garden. He is warned of the dangers of continuing the conflict. It is likely that if the fighting continues, the "garden" of France that he is fighting for will be destroyed. Henry agrees a peace treaty with the French. He courts Princess Katherine of France and agrees a peace treaty with her country. So the play ends. The parallel in the modern world is the obsession that many organizations have with "preparing for battle"—rationalizing, re-engineering, de-layering, downsizing to get lean. As a result, they lose good people and morale is severely impacted. This aggressive, warlike approach to business can deliver results in the short term, but in the medium and long term it can lead to burn-out and loss of the most talented people.

Inspiration

We began by acknowledging that *Henry V* is the Shakespeare story that offers more learnings about inspiration than any other. So it is only right that we end with the best-known speech from the play (Act 3, Sc. 1). As we consider Henry's oration to his troops, we will draw out the elements that make it an outstanding example of motivating a workforce who are tired, frustrated, and beginning to lose belief in their ability to succeed.

The background is that Henry and his army have been fighting outside the town of Harfleur for three months and have lost 2000 men. Another 3000 are ill, and the remaining 5000 are beginning to experience strong feelings of doubt. He now has to rouse them to go back into battle: "Once more unto the breach dear friends." He addresses them as his friends; they are in this together.

> In peace there's nothing so becomes a man
> As modest stillness and humility,
> But when the blast of war blows in our ears,
> Then imitate the action of the tiger.

As Richard Olivier points out, it takes a different type of energy to be successful in war than it does in peacetime. In describing the characteristics of peaceful behavior, he reminds them of the outcome of the victory in war, that which makes it all worth it.

Henry also describes to his men how they will be successful in battle through powerful use of imagery:

> … imitate the action of tiger
> Stiffen the sinews, conjure up the blood,
> Disguise fair nature with hard-favoured rage.
> Then lend the eye a terrible aspect,
> Let it pry through the portage of the head
> Like the brass cannon, let the brow o'erwhelm it …
> Now set the teeth and stretch the nostril wide,
> Hold hard the breath, and bend up every spirit.

To re-motivate them, Henry reminds them of their heritage, their ancestors, and urges them to make their parents proud.

> On, on, you noblest English …
> Dishonour not your mothers; now attest
> That those whom you called fathers did beget you.
> By copy now to men of grosser blood,
> And teach them how to war. And you, good yeomen,
> Whose limbs were made in England, show us here
> The mettle of your pasture; let us swear
> That you are worth your breeding—which I doubt not,
> For there is none of you so mean and base
> That hath not noble luster in your eyes.

He finishes by describing them motivated, ready for battle, and draws their attention to the cause they will serve

> I see you stand like greyhounds in the slips,
> Straining upon the start. The game's afoot.
> Follow your spirit, and upon this charge
> Cry, "God for Harry, England and Saint George."

The workshop ends. Once more into the bar! This should be fascinating, as I have arranged for us to meet several people who have already participated in workshops run by Olivier Mythodrama Associates and have agreed to talk to us about what they have learnt.

There waiting for us is Andy, who is a regional director for a large retail bank. He is responsible for more than 30 bank branches employing over 300 staff.

He tells us how he first became familiar with the story of *Henry V* when he attended a course on leadership organized by the Cabinet Office. It was a program aimed primarily at people in the public service, and a small number of people from the private sector had also been invited. Richard Olivier ran a half-day session on leadership. Andy explains:

Listening to him describe the story of Henry made me realize that I needed to find more time for myself. At key stages before the battle, Henry had taken himself off on his own to consider what was happening around him and what it meant and how could he make it work. This had a major influence on me, and I now regularly find time for myself, in the middle of the day, even if it's only 15 minutes, to take stock of how I've spent my time and what I have achieved against what I had planned. If I hadn't spent time on things I had planned, I would ensure that I fulfilled those commitments I had made to other people. That is something I have since put into practice and the quality of my decisions has improved as a result.

Andy continued:

We all have our own styles and have to adapt. I learnt that I had to adapt my style with the same person in different situations. I had a direct report who was performing well and all that was needed was to give him regular praise and encouragement. This individual then moved into another role, which was a stretch for him; in that case, he needed more direction.

The other thing I realized was that you can have all the operating structures in the world, but you have to be able to articulate where you want to go and do it in such a way that people buy into it, otherwise you won't succeed, as Henry did.

I have since brought Richard in twice to work with two different teams. What I noticed afterwards was that they were making a bigger effort to win hearts and minds and that their people were responding much better to them.

Next we talk to Jane. She is a senior civil servant. She participated in a workshop that Richard ran on the public service leadership scheme. She describes the experience for us:

The major lesson for me in the Henry story was the realization that if you are involved in a change program, if you have your own project to win France, you can't muddle through, you must consciously think and act. Here we have people whose concerns I have to address, here I need to show sympathy. Try to step back occasionally. Pressures of everyday work make it difficult to take time out and assess the situation.

This experience has influenced my style. In my role, I do a lot of feedback of people who have been through promotion boards: some successful, some unsuccessful. I now frame my approach to these meetings as a "performance." I prepare carefully so that I can communicate clearly and effectively and also create a climate of trust where the person I am working with feels that they are being listened to, is able to express their own feelings about the decision affecting them and get valuable lessons from the experience. I think about my body language, create more pauses, opportunities for the other person to digest what I have said and make their own comments and raise questions and concerns as they occur. I have just done a round of debriefing candidates following promotion boards. I felt that candidates were responding well to me and indeed, one candidate told me that the feedback I gave her was the best she had ever received.

We are now joined by Geoff. Much of his career had been spent in the police service where he was a divisional commander. For much of his police career he had been responsible for the training and development of senior officers, including a period when he was director of the "high flyers" program. He left the police service a few years ago and now works as a consultant. Geoff introduced the *Henry V* work to senior officer training, having experienced it on a public service leaders program. He had noticed that people were tremendously enthusiastic about it. Over the three years, they considered it the best thing they had done. Participants have said that it helped them re-engage with their motivation for working in public service. It also helped some participants understand the differences in style between them and their boss.

Diane has a very interesting story to tell us about how *Henry V* had a major impact on the leaders in her organization. She is chief executive of a health trust, and this is her story:

> Seven years ago, we decided to explore unusual places to help us in developing our senior people and our organization. It is full of clinicians, who are brilliant doctors, but set in their ways and lacking insights about how to lead people. They can be a difficult group to work with. As if things weren't challenging enough, a decision was made to merge our hospital with seven others. We embarked on a program to integrate the organizations and get the people in them working together. As well as running seminars we did a leadership development course. OMA was part of a two-year program for consultants, GPs and nurses. Its purpose was to help them to equip themselves with the skills to lead people.
>
> As a result of engaging with Shakespeare's work in this way, I've seen a real change in the way people deal with others and an increase in awareness about the impact of how they treat others. We did *The Tempest*. We acted out parts of the play. In the big storm, the most senior people took the roles of the deckhands. It helped us realize that in a crisis, we can treat people really badly. People can do *Henry V* and then understand better how they need to act differently as leaders in different situations. They realize they can get things done in different ways.

It's not only *Henry V* that can provide valuable lessons for people working in today's organizations. Diane described how *The Tempest* helped managers in her organization appreciate the impact on their people of the way they implemented change.

In my own case, Shakespeare's play *Hamlet* has been a source of learning that has influenced my approach to work and colleagues. A few years ago I participated in a workshop based on the play, at Shakespeare's Globe Theatre in London. In the morning David Whyte, the poet and writer, asked us what was the part of us that we left behind when we stepped into our workplaces each day, and what was the impact of that loss?

I had no ready answer, and it returned to me again as we were given an exercise just before lunch. This was the task: we were each given a copy of the text of *Hamlet*. We were asked to look through it over the lunch break and select one or two lines that were meaningful to us. When we came back we would each read these lines aloud to the group and try to convey the meaning that it had for us. I immediately felt a pang of anxiety. How was I to do this?

At least we weren't coming to it completely cold. In the morning we had an overview of the story of the play and had discussed selected passages. I skimmed over the pages, but nothing jumped out at me. Then I recalled David's question: what is the part I leave behind in the morning when I come to work? I remembered how I had been touched in the morning when we had talked about the graveyard scene where Hamlet comes across the grave of Ophelia, who killed herself after going mad. Hamlet is angry over the nonchalant way the gravediggers are doing their work, singing and bantering while they dig. One of them digs up the skull of Hamlet's father's jester Yorick. Hamlet picks up it and acknowledges it with the words, "Alas, poor Yorick, I knew him … a fellow of infinite jest." Hamlet has a sentimental affection for the deceased jester, who played with him as a child and amused the boy with games, pranks and songs. So after lunch, I recited those words, in the realization that the part of me I often leave behind is that sense of fun.

Working in financial services, it's about serious things, like money. It's also about relationships, and as we spend a lot of our time there it needs to be enjoyable. So this was an important lesson for me, and since then I have given myself permission to engage others more in a sense of fun, to look for the funny sides of situations, to encourage my colleagues not to take themselves too seriously. I have had feedback to reinforce this change in approach.

The bell goes again for the end of this interval, and on that positive note we head back up into the theater for the next item in our program. It is a poetry workshop in which people from business will be reading and talking about poems that have been sources of learning and inspiration.

The first work we will hear is the poem "A doodle at the edge" by William Ayot, from his book *Small Things That Matter*, and it is read by Elizabeth, who is chief executive of a local authority.

A Doodle at the Edge

Another meeting, another agenda, another
list of buzz-words, initials and initiatives
PSU is entering Phase Three
while the CDR wants G2 to go to Level Five.

If we go the full nine yards on this one;
if we get pro-active, get out of the box, get
our teams together and on the same hymn sheet;
if we hit the ground running, if we downsize HR,
if we get the money onboard, and our asses into
*   gear,*
then we can change something, make a
*   difference,*
change what the other guys changed last week.

Meanwhile the god has left the garden,
the muse lies minimised in the corner of our
    screens.
Not dead, not buried, but ignored and unseen,
like a doodle at the edge of an action plan

Me? I say make a sacrifice to the doodle;
pick some flowers, speak a poem, feed the tiny
    muse.
Draw, paint, sing or dance, and you'll bring the
    gods
back into the board room; the laughing, smiling,
weeping gods of the night-time and the wild.

William Ayot

Elizabeth tells us how the last verse resonates strongly for her:

> It legitimizes being different in the way of doing things. I have a leadership profile, based on an assessment of my competencies. It is a rational, analytical model defining the competencies I should display. I can tutor myself to work according to that model, but I am a values-based person. This poem helps me get in touch with what is important to me and inspires me to be more creative in the way I do my job. I see myself as a creator of public value rather than an implementer of our statutory duties and achiever of numerical targets. I accept the importance of analysis in management and I also want to raise the importance of values in management. So "A doodle at the edge" reinforces my determination to create freedom and opportunities for the communities my organization serves rather than just manage resources or implement central government directives. William's poetry touches some deeply held and complex values within me and prompts me to evaluate my purpose as a CEO, which is something all leaders should do.

William Ayot does a lot of work with people from business, and he noticed that managers tend to fall back on jargon when they are presenting. "A doodle at the edge" is about that tendency, and a challenge to speak more from the heart. Jargon does have some value but it doesn't move people. Much of the language used in organizations is dull, flat, and at best merely informs. This poem brought into Elizabeth's awareness her belief that her work should be about creating values for communities rather than simply executing government directives, represented by the sterility of organization jargon. It stimulated her to evaluate her purpose and to move on to something more meaningful.

William Ayot hopes that his poems will increase the visibility of leaders. He says that leaders get covered in post-it notes: expectations. But are they prepared to take them off and reveal who they are? In his work with rehabilitation of prisoners, he discovered that men were able to access difficult issues through poetry. In prisons he would read a poem and the men could access the feelings that were common to many of them. Many of the men were obsessed, and they were driven, as are many people in business. In his boarding school experience, expression of emotion was discouraged. He worked in the gaming industry and tried to adopt the poker face. He and his colleagues were encouraged to shun and shut down emotion.

He argues that emotion is vitally important, but the very language and structure of work can create alienation. A way back to emotions is though poetry. Poetry can bring us back in touch with nature. We are now so focused on targets we tend to shut down the senses. When we focus less, the senses come alive and we become more creative. The softer our focus, the more creative we become, and the more in touch with our emotions. Confucius said: "Before we can rectify society we have to rectify language." William describes his mission as trying to recapture words and bring them back to the workplace.

The second and final poem we will hear is another by William Ayot, again from his *Small Things That Matter* collection. It is poem that is addressed to us all: leaders and followers, and it is read by Alastair, a director of a telecommunications company.

The Contract (A word from the led)

And in the end we follow them
not because we are paid,
not because we might see some advantage,
not because of the things they have
    accomplished,
not even because of the dreams they dream
but simply because of who they are:
the man, the woman, the leader, the boss
standing up there when the wave hits the rock,
passing out faith and confidence like lifejackets
knowing the currents, holding the doubts,
imagining the delights and terrors of every
    landfall;
captain, pirate and parent by turns,
the bearer of our countless hopes and
    expectations.
we give them our trust, we give them our effort.
what we ask in return is that they stay true.

William Ayot

Alastair tells us that he first heard the poem read by William at the launch of *Small Things That Matter* at Shakespeare's Globe Theatre in December 2003:

> I was sitting in the pit of that theater, albeit a replica, but experiencing the same conditions as theater goers would have 400 years earlier. It was cold. The rain drizzled down and William and friends stood on that famous stage reading to us. The aircraft passing low above on their way to Heathrow reinforced the connection with modern times, as we heard William's poems: "A doodle at the edge," "Career moves," "A change of culture," "The interview," "The heroes of everyday life," and "The contract." Poems capturing timeless themes of human dilemmas, relationships, and contradictions, in their descriptions of modern lives of business people.
>
> I bought a copy of the book on the night and spent time reading through the pages, on the homeward train journey. Everyone I shared these poems with was moved by them. Some were left uncomfortable. I felt inspired particularly by "The contract." For me it is the most succinct and definitive statement of what leadership is all about. It speaks to me of courage, supporting others, honoring commitments to others and above all being true to the values that I express to others and more importantly I hold dear.
>
> There have been points in the last year where I have been faced with the challenges of responding to the unethical behaviour of colleagues. There was no easy or elegant way of dealing with these issues. Impulsively confronting those involved would have been damaging to some who had confided in me, yet I couldn't allow these actions to pass and I had to ensure that wouldn't occur in the future. It was then that I revisited "The contract." I realized that first of all the most important person I had to be true to was myself, to my own values.

I then mapped out a course asking myself at each stage whether I was being true to all those involved. When I was satisfied that these conditions had been met, I took action that addressed the issues and ensured that they could not be repeated. Since then, I have kept a copy of "The contract" in my desk to remind me of those characteristics of leadership. I have found that I have been better able than at any stage in my career to have challenging conversations. By keeping myself true, my sense of purpose has become clearer, my relationships with colleagues and particularly those who report to me have become stronger, and I have experienced greater loyalty than ever before.

We have spent an eventful time at this theater. We learnt how acting can help us develop our ability to think on our feet, instilling in us the discipline of preparation required for excellent performances. We revisited Shakespeare and discovered powerful lessons about leadership and motivation in the story of *Henry V*. Finally, in hearing about the poetry of William Ayot, we were reminded how the language of emotions in verse can inspire us to clarify our own sense of purpose and identity.

7
COMMUNITY

BEFORE WE VISIT the next place in our program, I want to share a personal learning with you. During my first year with Aon, I decided to organize a quarterly "leaders forum." This was to be an opportunity for the 100 most senior people in the company to learn from experiences of leaders in other business sectors. It was important that we got off to a good start, and a lot would depend on the quality of external speakers.

I had already booked an executive who had an impressive CV, having worked for one of the major international airlines. I had seen a video of him in action and met him. He was an accomplished presenter and I felt confident. We needed another speaker, and a colleague suggested someone who ran a charity in east London. Like me, she was fairly new to the company, and while she wasn't certain he would be a perfect fit, he was worth checking out. I was initially sceptical but agreed to see him.

His name was David Robinson and the meeting went well. He spoke authoritatively and clearly had experience of dealing with the private sector. On the night, I was naturally concerned that everything would go well at this our first leaders forum. While my instincts told me that there would be parallels between leadership in the voluntary sector and in business, I wasn't sure how compelling it would be for our senior people. Many of my colleagues had spent most of their careers in the insurance industry. It was important to stimulate their curiosity about how other businesses were led. Was I asking too much to expect them to get enthusiastic about leadership in the voluntary sector? I decided to manage the risk by having David speak first, so if we had a low-key response then I always had my speaker from business to follow.

I was still feeling a bit apprehensive as David was introduced. He was very assured: beginning by telling us that when he heard about the topic for this event (Inspirational leadership) he was reminded of Woody Allen extolling the virtues of speed reading who said: "I read *War and Peace* this morning in three hours. It's about Russia." David acknowledged the danger of dealing with such a vast topic in a similarly superficial way. My confidence grew. He then went on to describe the origins of his organization, its principles and purpose, and case studies of some of the people his organization had helped by providing a "ladder out of poverty."

David spoke with humility, sincerity, conviction, and a sense of humor, which struck the right chord. He acknowledged that his own experiences of leadership might seem far removed from ours, and asked us to bear in mind some of the background to the people he worked with. Here are a couple of examples:

Dan

Dan would describe himself as the generation in between, having lost both his parents and children in Vietnam before arriving independently in the UK. Prior to that he had never left his home region. Eventually he set about helping other Vietnamese refugees to establish themselves here. He now runs an organization with wide-ranging services for both the Vietnamese refugee community and others. Had Dan been born under other stars he would probably have had a leadership role in society. The fact he still lives in very modest circumstances in east London is more to do with his beginnings than his own talents.

Howard

Howard came to David's organization several years ago with a reference from his head teacher describing him as uneducated and uneducable. He became involved in an education program with school non-attendees, concentrating on literacy, numeracy, and IT, backed up by behavioral work with the family. After two years Howard was both literate and numerate and had become very involved in some work with younger children. Eventually he became a qualified youth worker and worked with the local authority. Recently he became an AA patrolman. Howard previously had a record for motoring offences. So, as he would say, he is still messing about with cars.

David then asked us to read his charity's statement of purpose:

> To generate change. To tackle causes not symptoms; find solutions not palliatives. To recognise that we all need to give as well as to receive and to appreciate that those who experience a problem understand it best. To act local, but to think global. Teach but never stop learning. To distinguish between the diversity that enriches our society and the inequalities that diminish it. To grow, but to build a network not an empire. To be driven by dreams, judged on delivery. To never do things for people but to guide and support, to train and enable. To simply inspire.

He then acknowledged my concern that we might be thinking his organization was tiny and so different from Aon that we could not see any point of contact. He challenged that if we changed maybe four or five words of his statement of purpose we would find it applicable to our business, because how we go about our activities is just the same.

He proudly told us that this statement of purpose adorned the walls of several companies who are involved with his organization, including a government department, a firm of city solicitors, and an investment bank. It resonates for them too, because the best ways of working are consistent whatever our business.

David was a hard act to follow, and while our business speaker did a competent job, he had been outshone on the night. At the Q&A David got better and better. Afterwards several people came over and congratulated me for finding such an inspirational presenter. At subsequent leaders forums, our Chairman and Chief Executive, Dennis Mahoney, referred back to David, saying what a great example of leadership he showed us with his passion and conviction.

So what was the learning for me? Well there were several. I was glad I had taken the risk of bringing in David. My apprehensions were based on the fact that he wasn't from the business world and this was the first time we had brought this group together, never mind them being addressed by an external speaker. There were several unknowns for me and the event was highly visible. There was a lot at stake for me. These leaders forums were a key element of our approach to leadership development. They needed to get off to a good start. I also knew that David was a good speaker and his message was relevant. My apprehension that the impact of his message could be diluted because it was based on experience in a different environment was ill-founded.

This experience reinforced my belief that there are universal lessons of leadership that transcend cultures. The key is in the skill of the speaker to deliver those messages in a compelling way that is relevant. One of the very effective things that David did was to acknowledge the differences between his world and ours. He also made these differences specific and encouraged us to look for the similarities. By doing this he created a climate of mutual respect and understanding, conducive to a desire to understand rather than refute. Subsequent leaders forums have been very successful, and it encouraged me to be bolder in my approach to leadership development, introducing many of the ideas that I discuss throughout this book.

David Robinson's organization is Community Links, which is a charity running community-based projects in east London and it is the next place we will visit.

Community Links

Community Links began in David Robinson's mother's back room in 1977 while he was at school and living in Newham in east London. It was and still is considered to be one of the poorest boroughs in England and Wales. The initial idea was born when David and some schoolmates got interested in developing youth activities in Docklands. In those days there were no permanent facilities. Fortunately they managed to acquire an old double-decker bus quite cheaply, and converted it into a playbus. The bus visited different sites from which they ran primitive play schemes and youth activities, which attracted up to 130 kids on a Sunday.

Community Links is a charity that now helps over 30,000 vulnerable children, young people, and adults every year, with most of the work delivered in the East London Borough of Newham. Its successes influence both community-based organizations across the United Kingdom and government policy. Activities include education programs for school non-attendees, family advice sessions, work with homeless young people, training schemes, counselling groups, and visits from the emergency services. In 2003, there were 130 permanent staff, 220 seasonal workers, and 400 volunteers across 60 sites in east London. Former service users deliver 80 percent of the frontline work.

What can we learn from Community Links? Well we can ask David Robinson to come and speak to us. We can read his recently published book *Unconditional Leadership* in which he has distilled the leadership experiences of Community Links into a "principle-centered approach to developing people, building teams and maximizing results." *Unconditional Leadership* contains useful ideas and techniques that can be used right away in a wide range of settings, and I will return to one of these before we move on.

In his speech to Aon's senior leadership group, David acknowledged the contribution to Community Links made by large prestigious corporations and professional firms. One of

118

these is Lovells, the top City law firm, which employs over 1000 lawyers in London. Seven years ago, Lovells initiated a *pro bono* scheme in partnership with Community Links. This provides free legal representation for people appealing against an unsuccessful application for disability allowance. If the allowance is granted, the government pays the individual approximately £15 a week. In addition, it is a "passport benefit," which means that eligibility enables the individual to be considered for other allowances. While there is a right of appeal against a rejected application, no legal aid is available. Community Links refers clients to Lovells, which then provides a lawyer to represent them at the appeal hearing, presenting new medical evidence. At the end of 2004 there were 80 lawyers in the firm trained to work on the scheme. Without the *pro bono* service provided, applicants would have to face the daunting process of appeal without legal representation. The national average success rate at appeal is 40 percent while with the Lovells/Community Links scheme there is a 77 percent success rate.

Yasmin Waljee, who is *Pro Bono* Manager of Lovells, describes how involvement in the scheme assists in the development of young lawyers:

> In addition to the obvious satisfaction of assisting someone in need, the Community Links training and practical experience of representing Community Links' clients complements our formal training and builds on the professional skills of our young litigators. As a result, they develop their judgment and practice, in particular with regard to case strategy, client file management, and advocacy.

So here we have a real win/win as lawyers are able to accelerate professional learning and the applicants have a higher chance of successfully appealing for a government allowance that can make a real difference to their lives. Here a young lawyer describes how involvement in the scheme also provided a sense of intrinsic satisfaction as well as providing a professional development opportunity:

> On Wednesday 20 August 2003 I made my first atten-dance on a Community Links client since starting at Lovells in July. The visit was to take a proof of evidence from the client in support of his appeal against the refusal to renew his application for Disability Living Allowance. The experience is very similar to and at once very different from any fee earning work that you will do at Lovells or any of the other City law firms.
>
> In order to win the appeal the appellant must satisfy the tribunal on the balance of probabilities that he is unable or virtually unable to walk. Winning the appeal will depend on the evidence adduced and submissions as to what the evidence means in the context of the legal tests. The principles are exactly the same as for cases heard in the Commercial Court every day.
>
> The point to emphasize is that we all know how a case, so sterile on paper, takes tangible shape as soon as the witness is seen in the flesh. Reading that someone takes five minutes to walk 30 yards is virtually meaningless compared to seeing someone requiring the assistance of two people to stand, their labored and lurching steps, pausing to regain balance and breath between steps, the fear as they stand in the small area of no man's land between the table and chair, momentarily adrift with no immediate support that they can grab on to. Suddenly the case becomes real.
>
> It is this reality that leads to the differences between the work Community Links do and what we usually do. Community Links' work makes a small but very real and

tangible difference to individual people who without our assistance would be far less likely to succeed and in any event find the whole process very daunting. The difference that success or failure of the appeal makes may seem meaningless, since an extra £20, £30 or even £100 a week might go unnoticed and if the worst came to the worst we could always abandon Pret's in favour of a less well-known sandwich shop or, god forbid, make them ourselves. However, for Community Links' clients the difference is at the very essence of their basic needs. Given that often they cannot walk, it is the difference between whether or not they can afford a taxi to take them out to buy their food.

After having successfully completed one of these cases I would defy anyone not to feel a sense of euphoria in a way that you may not experience in traditional City work. You will build your confidence as an advocate and as a lawyer by making decisions and seeing the effect of them. What you learn in terms of making personal judgments on evidence, tactics, and law; learning how to persuade a tribunal; determining whether a witness is honest, helpful, or concealing material facts will be equally useful in your more traditional work. Therefore, there is no doubt that you will become a better lawyer through taking on Community Links cases.

The Community Links/Lovells *pro bono* scheme is a great example of professionals discovering learning in an unexpected place. As the young lawyer described so eloquently: when you hear the story of the individuals involved, the case becomes real and as a result the learning you gain is more powerful. The same can be said for a story that David Robinson tells in his book *Unconditional Leadership.*

Pacing the change

He describes how in one of his first placements as a relief worker in a children's home he found himself working under a strict regime. The children were all under ten and not allowed to speak at meal times, while staff supervised them in silence. David and another colleague who was also new were uncomfortable with this approach. They felt that meal times were for sharing, and they should eat with the children and encourage them to talk. When David and his colleague were alone on duty with the children, they sat down to eat with them and started talking to them. Initially no one responded, then the noise level rose and things began to get out of hand. He describes the scene:

> Eventually children were shouting from one table to another. Then a chip went over my head, followed by more. Someone was under the table, someone was crying. It was already ending in tears and we hadn't begun the rice pudding.

David was deeply disappointed by this failure, and felt the children had let him down. The older staff had been dismissive of his aspirations, and now he questioned whether his beliefs about good residential social work were "naïve and impractical." He didn't resolve this dilemma during that placement but he did reflect on it a great deal. He noticed similar patterns when working with new colleagues who had been used to working in a very different environment. For example, civil servants seconded to Community Links struggled with a working environment that encouraged more responsibility than they were used to, and expected more innovation and required greater flexibility.

The children at meal times and the secondees had one thing in common. They had both lost the clear set of parameters that guided their customary living and working environments. They had no familiar reference points and weren't sure what was expected of them or to expect from others. They weren't sure what they could take for granted, what they could assume was normal. The impact ranged from a breakdown in order with the case of the children, and probably a combination of confusion and frustration on the part of the secondees. The lesson here is clear, in the words of Martin Luther King: "Social change won't come overnight. But we must always work as though it were a possibility in the morning." If we move too slowly, we lose momentum; too fast and we fail to win hearts and minds. This is particularly important point, as our private and business lives are continually buffeted by what seem like never-ending demands for change of some sort or another.

Interestingly, we came across a very similar discovery in the field of sports, when Lesley, a CEO of a health care business, drew on her experience as an international rower. You will recall that Lesley could only sustain change in her company over time if she accepted that every so often the pace had to be adjusted to allow key people in the organization to catch their breath and adjust to the new pace.

It is time now to move on, but before we do we should reflect on what a fruitful visit we have had to Community Links. We have learnt about the transferability of leadership principles. We have gained insights about managing change from observing others who have found themselves outside their comfort zones. It has also been revealing to discover how involvement in charitable work has been both developmental and inspirational for young professionals.

Where to next? We will travel now to the north west of England, to Liverpool.

Why am I bringing you to Liverpool? There are many reasons to go there, and on this occasion it is to visit the home of the Furniture Resource Centre (FRC). I met their former CEO, Liam Black, in the summer of 2004, and realized he had a great story to tell about the work this "social enterprise" was doing. It had already started a business called The Cat's Pyjamas to help people learn from their experiences, and I realized you could discover some great things by paying them a visit. The Cat's Pyjamas offers powerful insights into what it takes to achieve and sustain financial, social, and environmental returns from a business. And that's what a social enterprise is: a business that makes money whilst tackling social problems, for example, by creating job and training opportunities for unemployed people, helping the homeless, and tackling environmental problems.

So what about FRC? Who are they and how do they go about their "social business"?

In 1988 Nic Frances, a former stockbroker in his mid 20s, started the Furniture Resource Centre to provide furniture for low-income families. Since then it has grown from a handful of volunteers to become one of the country's best-known social businesses, with 60,000 customers and generating a turnover of nearly £5 million. Ten years ago, FRC was dependent on grants for 84 percent of its income. In 2003/4 only 7 percent was from grants and 93 percent of its income was from the sale of goods and services. FRC now runs several businesses described below:

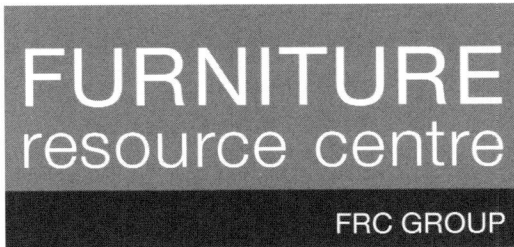

Furniture Resource Centre provides a service furnishing empty properties for social landlords, including local authorities and housing associations. Customers can order from a catalog everything from carpets, furniture, and curtains to cleaning equipment and even cutlery. In the last year, it helped transform 3500 empty properties into homes, improving the quality of life for people living in the area. This also helps the landlord by speeding up the re-letting process, reducing the costs of keeping empty properties.

Bulky Bob's is a great example of a business delivering financial, social, and environmental benefits. It collects bulky household items that its 50,000 customers no longer want, recycling and refurbishing 30 percent of everything. This includes thousands of items of furniture it refurbishes and sells at a discount to low-income families in FRC's Revive store in Liverpool. The social impact is obvious, and by diverting bulky items away from landfill it is making a positive contribution to the environment.

the cat's pyjamas

The Cat's Pyjamas is a joint venture that provides learning experiences about running a social business. It arranges for people to learn about best practice in the United Kingdom and internationally, including study tours to South Africa and the U.S.A. One event in San Francisco introduced FRC to the Ben and Jerry's PartnerShop, which provides a training scheme and attractive employment to disadvantaged young people, while also selling great ice cream! This inspired FRC to open Ben and Jerry's first PartnerShop in Europe in the center of Chester. The decision to sign the franchise agreement illustrates FRC's values in action. This was the first of their businesses whose product was not in itself a social or environmental benefit. You could argue that selling high-fat-content ice cream was socially irresponsible given widespread concerns about obesity. This challenged FRC to really question whether its businesses had to deliver good returns on all three bottom lines: financial, social, and environmental. It went ahead, and true to its values it took the opportunity to influence

Ben and Jerry's on supply chain and environmental issues. The coffee sold initially in the PartnerShop used a lot of plastic packaging and was not fair trade. So FRC persuaded Ben and Jerry's to change to a fair trade supplier, not only in the Chester shop but also in all its UK franchises.

A major objective of all FRC businesses is providing jobs and training to long-term unemployed people. Training contracts are offered to just under 50 people a year in logistics. As well as transferable skills and qualifications, trainees develop a work ethic that makes them more marketable when they leave. Success rates are high. Eighty percent of trainees successfully complete the programs and 70 percent of them go into jobs when they leave. While these statistics are impressive, it is the underlying care and commitment with which this training is provided that represents the true spirit of FRC. Don't get me wrong, FRC is a not a soft option and at times it has to take a "tough love" approach to supporting its trainees back into a working environment. So it introduced in 2003 "Here's the deal," which is in effect a contract with the trainee clarifying mutual commitments, requiring the trainee to turn up on time, treat his or her colleagues with respect and stick to the training plan. The vast majority succeed, and only a very few have had their contracts terminated.

Although the company will take a firm line when it is absolutely necessary, it does go out of its way to provide training opportunities. Support is provided to acquire job-related qualifications such as forklift truck driving licences. Qualifications are also offered in computer literacy and information technology, manual handling, health and safety, first aid, and essential food hygiene. Providing training is given a very high priority. This is reflected by the fact that FRC is prepared to take people on the logistics program who don't have a driving licence, even though they demand more time from other staff, cost more, and are less productive in the early stages.

FRC's "University of the People" costs £50,000 a year. Not spending that money in the last year would have enabled the group to make an overall profit. In its annual report it is made crystal clear that the decision to sustain this investment was made because FRC is not a furniture business. Rather it is about personal and social change, so spending on training in this way is central to the type of company it is.

The impact training has on unemployed people is put simply and powerfully by a trainee on completion of his induction:

> I'm more at ease with people and have a greater understanding of the working environment.

The growth of these businesses and their delivery of financial, social, and environmental benefits are impressive. What is also striking about them is the way they are run. FRC is a purposeful, values-driven organization that rigorously measures its performance and is wholeheartedly committed to learning. What can *we* learn from it? I believe a great deal. Its business model is very sophisticated and it has won awards for its approach to measuring social impact. But learnings really take on meaning when we hear the stories of real people and the insights they have gained from their experiences.

FRC had its fifteenth anniversary in 2003 and decided to mark that event, but not with a self-congratulatory publication heralding its greatest successes. Rather it wanted to produce something that was true to its values (professionalism, creativity, bravery, and passion), something that would reflect its commitment to openness and transparency and that would offer insights into how this social business was run. So it published *Fifteen Lessons Learned the Hard Way*. It is an engaging collection of stories that illuminates the journey of discovery that has been the development of FRC. These stories are extremely relevant for people in all walks of life, particularly those working in organizations and wanting to increase the contribution they make. Here are some examples of lessons FRC shared.

Flattering headlines and publicity should never influence sound business decisions

In 1998, FRC launched with a great deal of publicity Revive, a new retail store on the edge of Liverpool city center. The idea was that it would offer quality new furniture that would be bought by richer "middle classes" who would be attracted to buy their furniture from a social business. People on low incomes would be able to use the store through an arrangement with a credit union. In addition, unemployed people would get work experience and training in retail. But it didn't work. Middle-class people didn't use the shop. Difficulties with the credit union idea meant it never got off the ground. The furniture was too expensive for people on low incomes. In addition, there was a lot of local competition in the market.

The store started to make serious losses. But the FRC leadership continued to back the project. Consultants were brought in who argued that things could be turned around. Losses continued and eventually, FRC decided to cut its losses. Jobs were lost. Some people transferred to other jobs in the group. Furniture was sold off at a discount. The store was restocked with quality second-hand furniture to people on low incomes. Sales improved and the store hasn't looked back: since then it has consistently met or surpassed sales targets.

The group did however let the store run on the original pattern for three years. It should have repositioned the store much earlier, and as a result losses would have been much less. The launch of Revive had been very high-profile and in telling the story of Revive, Colin David of FRC explains how it is a salutary lesson why "flattering headlines and publicity should never influence sound business decisions."

Help and inspiration can come when you least expect them and from the most unlikely sources

Jim Donovan, now a board member of the FRC Group, was previously head of corporate affairs for Thorn EMI.

Thorn EMI, as owners of Radio Rentals and Rumbelows, was one of the largest retailers of white goods in the country, and a large proportion of its customers were low-income households. The company wanted to put something back into the community, and decided to get involved in recycling white goods and training long-term unemployed people. It was looking for a location in the north-west. On a visit to FRC, Jim met Nic Frances, who was then CEO of the FRC Group. Nic persuaded Jim of the merits of a partnership.

In 1994, partnerships between voluntary bodies and large corporations were rare. Many people in FRC at the time were reluctant to get involved with a large company and everything they believed an organization like that stood for. They were not sure if they could trust them. Nic Frances took Thorn's offer at face value and worked hard to convince his colleagues in FRC that Thorn could give them access to valuable resources and skills that wouldn't otherwise be available.

Create was launched in 1984 in an old warehouse in Liverpool. Since then it has trained hundreds of unemployed people and recycled thousands of white goods. The relationship between FRC and Thorn is still strong, and both organizations are represented on the board of Create. It wouldn't have happened if Nic hadn't seen the potential value in Thorn's offer and convinced his colleagues to take this opportunity to get help from what was considered at the time a most unlikely source.

Talent

You could argue that Steve Mostyn of Motorola was doing exactly that when he invited the former CEO of the FRC Group, Liam

Black, to talk to senior executives from his company. Motorola is a global leader in communications, employing approximately 100,000 people in 1000 locations across six continents, generating sales in 2003 just under $30 billion. Steve is responsible for leadership development, and runs an event twice a year called "Executive Trends." The top 300 leaders in the company are invited to hear global thought leaders present their ideas in a way that will challenge their assumptions about leadership.

Leaders in many corporations are now paying a lot of attention to the subject of talent management. That's because the capabilities of staff are increasingly seen as a source of competitive advantage, and managing that talent is now considered an important corporate priority. Steve was concerned that his company was looking at talent in a narrow way, assuming a scarcity of really good people and taking a very elitist view. He wanted to open up their minds to a different way of approaching the challenge. He therefore arranged for Liam Black to address this senior group of executives in Chicago.

Liam's approach contrasts starkly with the elitist view of talent as a scarce commodity. He described how FRC deliberately targets people who are long-term unemployed with limited formal training and education. The philosophy is that there is an abundance of talent out there, and they just have to create the right conditions to enable people to fulfill their potential. This is exactly what FRC is all about, while there is a tendency for companies to think about talent as a scarce asset. This attitude has been encouraged by Ed Michaels, Helen Handfield-Jones, and Beth Axelrod, who work for the management consulting firm McKinsey, and published a report in 2001 on *The War for Talent*.

Yet the approach that Liam Black and FRC have towards developing talent is closer to the original meaning of talent. To find that we have to go back to the Book of Matthew in the New Testament. At that time "talent" was a coin or unit of currency. According to the parable of the talents, a man who has three slaves is about to go on a journey and entrusts his money to them. He gives each one some talents and after a long while returns. Two of the slaves have invested the talents, doubling their master's money, for which he is most grateful and rewards them. The third slave was afraid and hid the talents given to him in the ground. He is only able to return the master his original investment. The master is angry and takes this slave's talents and gives them to the other slaves, casting the unprofitable slave into the darkness.

So it is not that talent is scarce. Rather there is an abundance because talent is really another way of saying we have untapped potential. And if the success FRC achieves with unemployed people is anything to go by, it is opportunities to develop talent that is scarce rather than natural ability.

This also a key part of the philosophy of the Delancey Street Foundation in San Francisco, which is the next place we shall visit.

Delancey Street Foundation

The Delancey Street Foundation believes that while Harvard serves the needs of the top 2 percent in society, it exists to serve the bottom 2 percent. It has pioneered what it describes as "an entrepreneurial pathway out of poverty." Founded in 1971 by Mimi Silbert and her partner, the late John Maher, Delancey Street has been transforming lives ever since. When a resident arrives at the foundation, he or she will typically have had a substance abuse problem for 10 years and been in prison four times. Over 40 percent have been homeless. When participants leave, they re-enter society as self-sufficient citizens. Over 20,000 have graduated from the foundation.

People joining the foundation are asked to make a two-year commitment. The doors aren't locked, and participants may choose to leave at any time. Most stay for three or four years. They start at the bottom, doing chores such as sweeping, mopping, and looking after the facility's parks.

The emphasis is on taking responsibility and operating on an "each one teach one" basis. Participants quickly progress to more responsible jobs where they oversee newer arrivals. First goal is the high-school equivalency certificate. This is quickly followed by hands-on experience in Delancey Street's training businesses, including a removal business, automotive business, and a highly rated restaurant. When they are ready to leave, participants have received the equivalent of a high-school diploma and training in at least three job skills. They have also had plenty of opportunity to supervise and develop their management talents. Sixty percent come from the criminal justice system on parole and about a third have been homeless. The emphasis is on taking responsibility and helping fellow participants to do the same. The ground rules are clear: no violence, no threats of violence, and no drugs or alcohol. Remarkably, the organization's history is unmarred by violence.

Like FRC in Liverpool, Delancey Street is not a charity. It's a social enterprise with three main aims: to make a profit and be financially self-sufficient; to have a positive social impact; and to have a positive impact on the environment. Self-sufficiency is so important because it allows the enterprise to set its own agenda, and allows it to scale up to grow. When you have to lumber through the government grant bureaucratic process, you can't plan. Nor can you predict with any accuracy what your income is likely to be when you are dependent on the whims of corporate executives about which good cause they will support this year. That's why these enterprises need to be independent, and that's what fuels their success.

Top Dog

Delancey Street is another moving story of disadvantaged people taking responsibility and transforming their lives. It is a story worth telling, but why have I brought you here? Rather than answer this myself right away, let's put this question to Adrian Simpson. Adrian is a Director of ?What *If!*, an innovation company that works with organizations to help them release the creative potential of their people and products. ?What *If!* takes business executives on Top Dog, which involves visits to leading international organizations in highly diverse sectors, ranging from aeronautics to health care. The thinking behind Top Dog is that for senior people intellectual argument alone is not enough, and that's why it creates these opportunities for them to see, feel, probe, and question.

Companies recently included on the tour are Southwest Airlines, Lockheed Martin, Stew Leonard's, The Ritz-Carlton, Griffin Hospital, Xlink, and Continental Airlines. Over 200 senior executives have already taken Top Dog tours, including well-known business leaders. This is a very impressive list of well-known international corporations. So why does Adrian include in such a program a visit to what many would consider an unexpected place like Delancey Street Foundation in San Francisco?

Adrian explains that he hears business executives talk a lot about the importance of aligning people's behavior with a vision, and of changing behaviors across organizations. He believes Delancey Street is the most extraordinary example of transforming people's behavior he has ever come across. It takes people on the bottom rung and transforms them into people with self-respect and skills. If it can be done with the people from Delancey Street with their backgrounds, then what is possible with the people you have in your organization?

There's another point, and it is linked to the one we discussed earlier about the abundance of talent. He points out that when we talk about the type of people at Delancey Street, with criminal records and histories of drug addiction, we tend to have preconceptions about what they will be like. Yet when you arrive at the Foundation, you actually meet intelligent, articulate people. Then you have to remind yourself that they have a history of deprivation and crime. When this happens we realize how incredibly judgmental we are. Adrian hears Top Dog participants talk about it. If you put a minor shoplifting offence on your job application form, in many cases you could be excluded from talent pools forever. Delancey Street shows what's possible and that's why every time the Top Dog tour goes there, Adrian sees many seasoned business professionals shed a tear or two, moved by the stories of personal transformation.

8
HOME

WE'VE TRAVELED far together; to some interesting places, met some fascinating people, and gained I hope some valuable insights. It's time to go home now. You may be ready to stop and reflect on what you've discovered on our journey, and consider where you would like to explore in the future. I hope you are keen to do this, and I will encourage you to think about that in more depth and do some planning before we part company. But you will have to wait a bit for that yet, as we have some more people to meet and discoveries to learn about.

So the final place we visit is my home, and as before I have arranged for you to meet some friends of mine. The discoveries they are going to share with us are based on what they have learnt from children.

Putting things into perspective

Frances is a very successful business developer, selling large IT systems and software to major financial services companies. She tells us that being a parent has had the biggest impact on her career. Time management, multi-tasking, and juggling skills have become the most important aspects of her life. As a result she has become more efficient at work, more objective, and somewhat more detached, as there is life beyond the office. She is actively involved with her daughter's riding career, and spends nearly all her free time with her at pony club and riding club events. Her professional life now has to fit in with her lifestyle, and funds it, rather than the other way round.

Frances finds that because of her professional skills she is asked to join committees of sports clubs, so that they can utilize her communication and organizational skills. So what started out to be her daughter's hobby has turned into a second major commitment. Coming to work is more like a "rest" after the busy commitments at home and during the weekends.

Parenthood has certainly meant she has become better organized and more efficient. But this may seem like just swapping one source of stress for another. There have, however, been other important benefits, as Frances describes:

> When I became a mother, I wanted to get home at the end of the day, so I stopped wasting time. Having children has also helped me get things into perspective. Before I had children, I would wake up in the middle of the night worrying about a project. Since I had children, that doesn't happen. I have responsibility for my children and ultimately that comes first. Work becomes more of a means to an end rather than an end in itself.

While Frances found that being a mother helped her get work into

141

perspective, Martin, a communications manager with an international bank, makes the point that his children challenge him to put himself into perspective. He explains:

> As you live your life, there is a risk that you become disconnected with what's important to others, as you establish your own perspective on the world. Even if you empathize with others, you realize that you have become more egocentric. And children are extremely egotistical. They cry when they are hungry. They don't discuss it with you. They fill their nappies [diapers] because that is what they need to do. They are not concerned about the impact on anyone else. My children continually remind me, and in so doing warn me, of my tendency to become egocentric and lose sight of what is important to others and the impact I have on them.

Philip Sorensen builds on this theme. He takes it a stage further as he believes that our family responsibilities put our whole lives into perspective. Philip is Chairman of Group 4 Securicor plc, a leading international security services company operating in 100 countries worldwide and employing over 340,000 people. He believes the challenges of running a family are very similar to those of running a business, and his responsibilities as a father and grandfather have been great sources of learning.

He tells us that he was reminded of this when his mother died, realizing that "everything was on loan." In other words, you are only granted stewardship for a temporary period. Here he elaborates on what he means by this:

> When your grandchildren are born, your own children become responsible for the next generation. You realize that you only have a temporary role in the circle of life. Being a parent means you must consider the impact of

your actions on the whole of the family for the future as well as for the present. As you only have these responsibilities for a temporary period you must encourage your children to adopt certain ethical standards, who in turn will do this for their own children. I believe you can apply similar principles to business. Again as your stewardship is only temporary: you must act in such a way to maintain the well-being of the whole of the business and ensure that important standards are maintained and adopted by successive generations of management and staff. You find that the beliefs that shaped your business career are same beliefs that guide you as a parent.

Carpe praesens!

While the family responsibilities of Frances, Martin, and Philip have helped put things into perspective for them, Andy who has been in sales his entire career since leaving university, has discovered his children role-modeled attributes that are critical to success in his profession.

The story that Andy will tell us now is one that he has used on several occasions to inspire his teams, who sell very sophisticated technology to large international companies.

He takes up the story:

> A few years ago, the "Game Boy" handheld game console was one of the favourite toys for boys. All three of our sons were desperate to have one. My wife Emma and I were reluctant to indulge this whim for an electronic gadget, and had resisted the pleadings, encouraging them to play sports and other outdoor games.
>
> One morning, I arrived at work as usual, starting what I expected to be a normal day: a planning meeting, one-to-one with a team member, and a presentation to a major client. My mood changed dramatically when I received a call from the police. I was told to go to the general hospital near my home, right away. Emma and the children had all been injured in a serious road traffic accident. As you can imagine, I had the drive through Hell to the hospital.
>
> Arriving there, I parked on a double yellow outside the main entrance and rushed straight in. My chest tightened as a nurse then ushered me into a room where Emma and the three boys were in bed. They all had neck braces and were heavily bandaged, but thankfully they were all conscious. I rushed over to Emma's side to check she was OK. She told me quickly that it

had been terrifying. As they had slowed down to turn off the main road, a truck traveling very fast had hit them from behind. Our car went out of control and rolled over three times, ending up on its roof. She bravely told me to go over and speak to the boys as they had all been shaken up by the crash.

I went over to the bed where Joseph, our eldest, was lying. He was badly cut and bruised. His limbs were swathed in bandages. I bent over carefully and gently asked "Joseph, are you OK?" He turned towards me and looked straight into my eyes and said, "Yes Dad, I'm fine, and can I have a Game Boy?"

All three had Game Boys within the hour.

Joseph got the result he wanted and Andy realized that his son could teach him a thing or two about persistence and single-mindedness. But why have I given this story the title *Carpe praesens*? You will have probably seen the film *Dead Poets Society* starring Robin Williams as a schoolteacher who motivates his class to fulfill their potential by taking the opportunities that life has to offer. He exhorted these boys to "*carpe diem*," or "seize the day." Andy's son, Joseph was an excellent role model for "*carpe praesens*" or "seize the moment," and that's what he did so well, even in the trauma of extreme adversity.

Transferable skills

While Andy identified capabilities in his son that are very valuable in a business environment, Graham and Robert both discovered how they could put their management skills to use for the benefit of their children.

Graham is a senior executive in a professional services firm. He tells us how he has learnt along the way to motivate his children, using his experience as a manager. He has found that handling some delicate situations with his sons has refined skills which have helped him be more effective in business. He believes that in many ways dealing with staff and colleagues is not much different from dealing with children. A particular case in point is how people learn to deal with failure—and how to become stronger as a result. Here Graham describes how he responded to his son's predicament:

> When my younger son, Jack, was 17, we had a real shock. Despite having worked hard, he got disastrous exam results. The boy was in tears. He didn't know what to do and didn't want to talk about it. Fortunately, I was able to use my experience as a manager to help him through this. Having acknowledged our disappointment I persuaded him to stand back and explore the options available. He needed to understand what he could do differently, and decided to seek help.
>
> We were so shocked we had to confirm whether it was a mistake in the marking. I went with him to see his director of studies. He confirmed that the marking wasn't the problem and the results were accurate. Jack then went through the results in detail and was able to see where he could improve. It was mainly about improving his exam technique. He had an excellent understanding of his subjects but had failed to apply that

knowledge effectively in the exam setting. His teacher helped him put together a plan. Having worked hard on that, he achieved excellent results the following year and got into the university of his choice.

In a similar vein, this is how Robert, who is regional director of a retail bank used management techniques, particularly around goal setting and ambition, to motivate his daughter to achieve exam success:

> When she was 16, Amanda was preparing to take her GCSE exams. She wasn't motivated. She was finding maths very hard but her school just ignored the problem.
>
> I got right beside her. First we identified what she was doing well, no matter how small, and reminded her of these strengths to build her confidence. We then went through her material systematically, identifying different sources of references for the areas in which she was experiencing most difficulty. This worked, and with thorough preparation she got the second highest grade possible and finished third in her class. A real transformation considering she was in the bottom half at the start of the year.
>
> While I was naturally delighted at the outcome, my daughter's experience with her teachers did cause me to reflect on my approach to motivating people. I realized that there are occasions when I am not clear whether people who work for me really understand or are capable of what I am asking them to do. As a result I now test more for understanding. I ran a large network of retail bank branches, and there are times when my people need to do things that are boring but critical. By helping my daughter get a sense of accomplishment in studying a subject she did not enjoy, I helped her achieve good

results. I now spend more time acknowledging the progress made by my staff, particularly with those activities that are particularly repetitive or boring but nonetheless critical to the effective operation of the business. They have responded well, and have consistently surpassed expectations for efficiency and accuracy.

Confronting the truth

Jeff, who is marketing director for a consumer goods company, and Lesley, CEO of a health care company, have found that their children have often challenged their own behavior. This is Jeff's experience:

> I have learnt many lessons in dealing with my children that I have been able to replicate in the workplace. Consistency, honesty, fairness, and keeping an open mind are all important. I have two daughters aged 13 and 10. For instance, take the issue of swearing. They keep me on my toes. I tell them not to, then they hear me do it and point out I am not consistent. It's uncomfortable but no less valid a criticism coming from a child. In fact you could argue all the more important, as with young people you are a role model and need to set an example. So I keep an open mind with children and they continually amaze me with the good ideas they come up with. It also has to be the same in work, and I try to keep an open mind about the ideas that my colleagues come up with no matter what part of the organization they are working in.

Lesley's challenge from her daughter was less direct and less comfortable. She has to admit that at times she squirms witnessing some of the less attractive aspects of her own behavior that her daughter has apparently inherited:

> My daughter Emma is a chip off the old block. At times she can be competitive, even pig-headed. When she was 14 months old, we had a nanny. Emma took her socks off. Nanny responded very calmly, asking Emma to put them at the bottom of the stairs so that they could take

them up and put them in the laundry bin later. "No," shrieked Emma, stamping her foot, and she threw the socks across the room.

Witnessing that incident, I experienced a blinding flash of light. I know someone else who could behave like that. Me! Seeing the rawness and strength of her character, I realized the potential negative consequences if not managed properly. It made me realize that I would need to stay close to her, supporting her to find strategies to embrace other people's point of view and manage her own frustrations. It also reminded me of my own volatility, heightening my awareness of the triggers that could provoke an angry or belligerent reaction in me. As a result I am more careful in situations when those triggers are likely to be pulled.

Putting yourself in others' shoes

Neill, a partner in a financial services company, and Michael, chief operating officer of a satellite communications company, have been challenged in very specific ways by children. Rather than cause them to confront their own behavior, their experiences have reinforced the benefits of looking through children's eyes. They have challenged their assumptions that what is important to them is not always so important to others. This is a truism that is easy to forget in the hustle and bustle of our working lives.

Neill echoes this sentiment when he tells us that perspective is sometimes difficult to find in the business world, and above all his children have taught him that to gain understanding you need to see matters through the eyes of others. If at that point you determine the relative importance of the matter both to you and to other involved parties; you have developed a true sense of perspective. His daughters' desire for a pet dog brought this home to him:

> I had been holding out against getting a dog as I believed it would be a three-minute wonder. As a compromise, two years ago my wife bought the children a hamster. My eldest daughter then became an expert about these animals, including their life expectancy, which is two years. Shortly after his second birthday Smudge, our hamster, died. We put him in a shoe box and took great care to bury him quickly in a far corner of the garden. We wanted to avoid the children suffering the distress of seeing their much loved pet in a deceased state. Gathering the children together indoors, we sat them down by the kitchen table and announced, "We have some bad news. Smudge the hamster has passed away." We braced ourselves for the sobbing but there was silence. Then our eldest daughter stood and asked, "Can we have a dog now?"

So we got it wrong, and it is easy to make the wrong assumptions. Why did our ten-year-old daughter not even shed a tear for Smudge the hamster, yet burst into floods of tears when she wasn't allowed to wear her clip-on earrings on a Saturday afternoon? Children get upset at things adults don't, and laugh at things we don't find funny. One thing's for sure, you can never take anything for granted with them. As with business and life in general, you have to continually challenge your assumptions about what's important to others. So now we have a pet dog: a small one, a Scottish terrier.

While Neill's assumptions about what is important were challenged by his four daughters, Michael Butler, chief operating officer of Inmarsat, was inspired by the opportunity of communicating to a much larger family: the children of the staff who work for the satellite communications company. The challenge was simply to explain what they do to their families.

Inmarsat operates a constellation of satellites that extend mobile phone, fax, and data communications across the world. The company stands at the forefront of wireless telephony, with customers in 80 countries.

Working with such advanced technology requires dedication, but there is always a risk that you can become preoccupied with the cleverness of the technology itself. When Michael joined the company a few years ago, he wanted to encourage the staff to be more outward-facing, to put more emphasis on the contribution that they made to customers and society as a whole, as well as the cleverness of the technology they were working with.

Working closely with Debbie Jones, vice president of HR, they ran company open days, where staff were encouraged to bring their wider families in to see how the business operated, and to gain a better understanding of exactly where their fathers and mothers spent so much of their time, what they did there and what the benefits for customers were. It was quite a challenge to present complex technology and services in a way that was understandable and interesting to children. The open days were a great success, featuring large colored pictures of satellites and a real spaceman. Given the cleverness of the work that Inmarsat staff do, it was very appropriate that there was a wizard in attendance, who proved very popular, keeping the children and their parents entertained throughout the day.

In 2002, Lord Sainsbury, the UK Government Minister for Science opened Inmarsat's new London Satellite Control Centre. In his speech he said:

> Inmarsat has consistently demonstrated itself to be a leader in exploiting commercial opportunities which come from space. We need more companies to follow Inmarsat's example of turning technology into "down to earth" services.

The family open days were great examples of communicating in a down-to-earth way. Inmarsat's marketing teams are also applying this principle, as they find new, simplified ways to communicate the features and benefits of their services to distributors and customers. Overleaf is an example from a recent advertising campaign showing how a ship's crew can take advantage of low call rates.

This has been a refreshing development for an organization well known for taking pride in the sophistication of the underlying engineering and technology of its satellite network. In the past even marketing people had a tendency to emphasize the complexity of what the company did.

It seems that helping children to learn about how Inmarsat helps get messages across the world helped the company learn how it could get its own messages across in a more down-to-earth way.

We have now completed our journey together. I hope you have

enjoyed visiting the places I have chosen for you, and found the people we have met stimulating. It is now time for you to begin to imagine what journeys of discovery you will embark on. We shall continue this conversation in the final chapter.

9
WHAT WILL
YOU DISCOVER?

NOW I HAVE introduced you to several people who have discovered some fascinating learnings in unexpected places, I hope you are now ready to plan some journeys of your own. My role has been to act as your guide as we visited new places together. Now I will encourage you to pause and reflect on what you have learnt on our journey together. In particular, consider what insights you have gained about how you can discover learnings in familiar places where you wouldn't necessarily expect to. And are there new places you want to visit that offer you the potential for discovery?

In the first chapter I invited you to invest in the high–yield, low–risk investment opportunity that is discovery. I pointed out that to realize the benefits of this opportunity, in many cases you hardly needed to do much more at all. That is because you are already doing many of the things that are required to make these investments. You are likely to be going to one or more of the places that we have visited together. It may be the cinema, going to the theater, watching sport, visiting art galleries, or listening to music. You may be a more active type, playing a sport or a musical instrument. Amateur dramatics may be your hobby, or painting or singing in a choir. Your weekends may be spent helping a local community group or working for a charity. You might have a hobby or interest we haven't talked about, or be a parent juggling the demands of work and family.

Discovery is not the only way that you will learn. There will be professional qualifications you will want to acquire. Companies and professional bodies will require you to attend formal training courses, particularly to gain specialist knowledge and specific expertise. Discovery is low–risk because the investment is small. To gain the benefits you don't have to spend a lot of money, nor do you have to spend any more time away than you would normally from your colleagues, friends, or families. All you have to do is adopt a different approach to the activities that you typically engage in. We shall look at that in some more detail shortly.

I am confident discovery works, having heard the stories of the successful people we have met together. They include highly successful entrepreneurs and accomplished executives holding major positions of responsibility in global corporations. We met sportsmen and women who have represented their countries, and men and women working in communities helping to transform the lives of disadvantaged people, who have as a result rediscovered a sense of purpose and their self–respect.

You may not have any of the hobbies or interests of the people we met together. You may not be a parent. Right now, time might be too short for you to have a hobby, but you still have opportunities for discovery. That's because there is potential for learning in everything you do, in all aspects of life. It is all around; you just have to approach life differently as a discoverer. It's time now to think about how you will do that.

How will you discover?

Your discoveries will be:

- driven by curiosity

- illuminated by insights

- realized through focused application.

How will you:

- become more curious?

- develop powerful insights?

- effectively apply these insights?

The answer is that you will do it in your own way. I won't be giving you a recipe or formula guaranteed to produce perfect results every time. That wouldn't be true to the spirit of discovery, and anyway we all know that there is no best way. There is only your way, the way that's right for you and that you are ready to follow at a given point in time. So, to help you develop your own approach to discovery, I am going to take you back briefly to some of the places we visited earlier and encourage you to consider carefully what was actually happening.

Meaningful experiences

We shall first go back to the cinema. You will recall Swag showed us an excerpt from the film *Gandhi*. This film was meaningful to him. There was a strong personal connection, as he watched it with his parents who were both born in India. Remember him telling us that his father was just about to go to university at the time Gandhi was assassinated. Then he described that scene at the salt works where the protestors were beaten down by the soldiers. Just as one protestor fell down, another came forward to take his place. This scene ended with an American journalist filing the story to his magazine, beginning with the statement that whatever moral ascendancy the West held, it was now gone.

There is much to be discovered in Richard Attenborough's great film. It showed how one man's personal beliefs could transform a nation's politics. It was Gandhi's powerful use of symbolism, in particular his commitment to peaceful, non–violent non–cooperation that made the greatest impact on Swag. He was influenced most by the fact that this strategy deployed by Gandhi was successful because to a large extent his opponents had not encountered it before and did not know how to respond effectively. Swag then described to us how he applied the lessons from *Gandhi* to business in competing with the market leader in a soft drinks market.

What clues has Swag given you about how you might discover on your next visit to the cinema? First of all, you have to decide which film to watch. There will be a lot of encouragement, as film producers and distributors make great efforts through advertising to attract your interest. But just because you have decided to pay your money, either at the box office or across the counter when purchasing or renting a DVD or video, it doesn't mean you are really going to pay attention to it. *Gandhi* had special meaning for Swag, watching it with his parents who were both born in India. There will be other facts about films that attract your attention. As well as location, the subject could be someone you have always admired, or the storyline could depict a challenge or situation that you have experienced or that someone close to you has. Whatever it is, pay attention to it and follow your instincts because that is what is stimulating your curiosity. And if you are curious you will engage, which is the first step in discovery.

Second, pay attention to your emotional responses to what's happening in the film, whether they be highs or lows, feelings of admiration or disgust, anger or frustration, joy or despair. Your emotional response is telling you what's important to you, just as Swag's did. Then afterwards as you are talking it over with a friend or loved one, you may comment on what moved you. If you are not the type that talks much about films afterwards, you may want to reflect. Whatever you do, ask yourselves some questions like:

- How did I feel when the hero/heroine said/did this/that?

- What would I feel if that happened to me or someone close to me?

- What would I do in that or a similar situation?

- What did a character that I really admired do in this film?

- Could I do that? When? How?

- What is likely to happen as a result?

- How can I learn more about that?

Or:

- Was there anybody in the film doing anything that I have done before?

- Was there anything happening in the film to someone that has happened to me?

- How were they different?

- How were they similar?

- What did they do differently?

- What was the result?

- What can I do differently next time?

Swag discovered in *Gandhi* what was important and meaningful to him. He applied his insights in business where he had a need to. That's what discovery is, and going through a process of questioning and reflection in the way I have described can guide you on your journey. Similarly, you will recall that Chris, who is sales director of a software company, talked to us about *The Godfather* and the advice given by Don Corleone to his son Michael. He told him to keep his friends close but his enemies closer. Rejecting the natural tendency to spend time with people who he got on with and avoid the others, Chris applied this principle in his dealings with a colleague who was resisting his initiatives. By each talking through their own priorities, they realized their aims were compatible. As a result they were able to progress without impeding each other's plans.

Again this is an example of someone taking something specific from an experience, gaining a powerful insight and applying it successfully. That is discovery in action.

Common factors

Another example was when Lesley, CEO of a health care company, realized that she had to "pace her organization" when introducing change. She gained insights while rowing for her university that she couldn't operate at peak performance all the time. Her coach used a technique which he called "wave training" whereby the rowing crew aimed to peak over a two–week period. They did so realizing that some of their times would be much slower than when performing at their best. It's common sense really. We can't always work flat out, to put it simply. But how often do we forget that when we are faced with a major challenge? This can be more accentuated when we face a competitive threat. So Lesley sowed some seeds for the need for additional change in her company at a time when they were already working on several initiatives. By engaging some key opinion formers, they then took up the mantle and started to push through some new initiatives when they and their colleagues were ready. The results were eventually very impressive, leading to significant gains in market share and profitability.

A similar insight about sporting performance was gained by Jeremy, commercial director of a publishing company. He drew parallels between fluctuations in sporting performance and those in business. When we visited the sports club, he argued that even great sports teams don't win every game. All sportsmen and women suffer slumps in performance from time to time. The same applies in business, and you need to bear that in mind when evaluating performance. He gave us the example of sticking with salespeople when their performance dipped. He found consistently that if they had been good performers in the past, they would do a good job in the future. He was invariably proved right, and so saved the company and individual the costly experience (in terms of money, morale, and productivity) of sacking a salesperson and hiring a replacement.

You could argue that it is easy to discover learnings in sport that can be applied in business. In the example given, the common factor is performance and how we respond to poor performance in particular. And that provides us with another clue about discovery. You will develop more powerful insights and identify greater potential for application in other spheres of your life if you ask the question:

> What does this situation have in common with other aspects of my life?

In Jeremy's case, performance was an important factor in both sports and business, and he was unsure initially how to respond to people whose performance was fluctuating. These two factors in common caused him to examine the underlying performance patterns of sportspeople, and then test whether similar patterns occurred in business.

Making it relevant

The theater, and in particular Shakespeare's plays, is a place that you might not have considered a source of discoveries that are relevant to business life. You may not even have been interested in Shakespeare at school. If you did study his plays you may remember long hours poring over the texts of the plays themselves and critical interpretation. Richard Olivier and his colleagues at OMA have brought this work alive for modern business people, and so facilitated the discovery of many business people, some of whom you have already met. OMA has framed or positioned the challenges of the characters in Shakespeare's plays in a modern sitting. This is very clear when you listen to how Richard describes Henry V's challenge in going to war with the French, using language similar to that used in a modern business:

> Henry V unites a group of disparate people (his nobles) around a common goal (reclaiming the territory of France) and manages to overcome all difficulties in his path to achieve a near–miraculous victory against the odds (winning the battle of Agincourt).

We are invited to see

> … the King as an inspired leader, the nation as an organization, the nobles as a senior management team, reclaiming territory in France as a big project …

By using language like this to describe or frame the challenges facing Henry, Richard makes the play more relevant and accessible to business people. A great example of this is when he describes the challenge that Henry faces in making the transition from reckless youth to respected monarch as "How to leave the pub." This is a dilemma commonly faced by many people when they have the opportunity to become a manager at a more senior level than friends they have regularly gone drinking with. There has to be some distancing to enable the new manager or leader to maintain some degree of objectivity, as well as having his or her own identity and not getting close to any particular group.

Positioning Shakespeare's characters like this in a modern setting enabled people like Andy, regional director of a retail bank, to discover the relevance of Henry V's challenges for them. Andy described to us how on the night before the battle, Henry had taken himself off on his own to consider what was happening around him and what it meant and how could he make it work. Andy told us that this had a major influence on him. He now regularly finds time for himself, in the middle of the day, even if it's only 15 minutes. He takes stock of how he has spent his time and what he has achieved against what he has planned. If he hasn't spent time on things he has planned, he will ensure that he has fulfilled commitments, particularly those he has made to other people. That is something he has since put into practice, and he believes the quality of his decisions has improved as a result.

What enabled Andy and others to develop the insight and apply them in their work environment was the way the story of *Henry V* had been positioned with the use of appropriate language in a modern setting.

The questions for you to bear in mind when seeking to discover are:

- How relevant is this character or situation to my world?

- How could I make them more relevant to my world?

- What changes could I make to the characters or their situations that would make them come alive for me and my colleagues?

- When I have done that what can I learn from their experiences?

Emotional response

When I described Swag's response to *Gandhi*, I suggested that you pay attention to your emotional response to the characters and events in a film. That normally suggests that it is touching something that is important to you. When this happens it often means there are potential discoveries in this area or around it. Poetry is often described as the language of emotions, and I raise that now to reinforce the potential for discovery in paying attention to your emotional response to a film, play or other experience. Elizabeth, who is a chief executive of a local authority, described to us how she was moved by "A doodle at the edge" a poem by William Ayot. Here it is again:

A Doodle at the Edge

Another meeting, another agenda, another
list of buzz–words, initials and initiatives
PSU is entering Phase Three
while the CDR wants G2 to go to Level Five.

If we go the full nine yards on this one;
if we get pro–active, get out of the box, get
our teams together and on the same hymn
     sheet;
Iif we hit the ground running, if we downsize HR,
if we get the money onboard, and our asses into
     gear,
then we can change something, make a
     difference,
change what the other guys changed last week.

Meanwhile the god has left the garden,
the muse lies minimised in the corner of our
     screens.
not dead, not buried, but ignored and unseen,
like a doodle at the edge of an action plan

Me? I say make a sacrifice to the doodle;
pick some flowers, speak a poem, feed the tiny
     muse.
Draw, paint, sing or dance, and you'll bring the
     gods
back into the board room; the laughing, smiling,
weeping gods of the night–time and the wild.

William Ayot

Elizabeth told us how the last verse resonated strongly for her, legitimizing being different in the way of doing things. This poem helped Elizabeth to get in touch with what is important to her, and inspired her to be more creative in the way that she does her job.

Your journal

As I have commented on each of these examples I have suggested questions that you can ask yourself to help you discover from your experiences. Whether you like to talk through experiences with other people or prefer to reflect quietly on your own, I recommend you keep a journal. Get one with a hardback, a good quality one for two reasons: you want it to last, and keeping your notes in a well–bound quality notebook symbolizes that what you write there is important to you. Only write in it when you are moved to. During some weeks, I make two or three entries in my own journal. Then four or more weeks can pass with no entries, followed by several pages in one day. To help your own discovery, write down what you are noticing in your work, in your daily travels, conversations, hobbies, and interests. Record what you are moved to write about. This should include what you are noticing about your response to situations or the response of others to you and to situations. Then spend a few moments reading what you have written and ask yourself:

- What is this telling me?

- What patterns do I recognize?

- Are events repeating themselves?

- Have I been here before?

- What is this saying to me about what I can do differently?

- What can I discover?

- What new places can I go to?

- What new things can I do?

- Will I?

- When?

- What similarities do I see in different situations and experiences?

- What does this tell me?

This may seem like a long list. Is what I am asking a bit vague? Perhaps you feel daunted by this. Is it a test to ascertain if you can truly discover? The answer of course is no. Only ask the questions you are moved to ask, and you will certainly only do that as far as providing answers are concerned. The important point to bear in mind about discovery is that it is your journey. You are completely in control and will decide where to go, how much attention to pay to each place, and what you will do next.

The spirit of discovery

This leads me to the final discovery I shall share with you, and it is one of my own. In 1950 a team of mountaineers from Scotland tackled the Himalayas. The account of the expedition was written up by W. H. Murray. There is a passage from it that has been quoted many times in books about leadership and personal development. I include it here because I have found it inspirational on many occasions: sometimes at work in facing the types of challenges that are part and parcel of business life. On one occasion there was something in my personal life that I was avoiding. Sitting in a colleague's office on a visit to London, I saw this passage on the wall. Having read it, a few minutes later I picked up the telephone and put in train a series of events that were to lead to a resolution.

I read it before I started on this project: the first book I have written. I can speak from experience: this message is prescient. My wife bought a framed copy on a business trip to Boston before we met, and gave to me when we were married. It's been around me for a while and I now hope it will inspire you to discover all that you can. Here it is:

Until one is committed, there is hesitancy,
the chance to draw back. Always ineffectiveness.

Concerning all acts of initiative (and creation),
there is one elementary truth,
the ignorance of which kills countless ideas and splendid
plans:
that the moment one definitely commits oneself,
then providence moves too.

All sorts of things occur that would never otherwise have
occurred.

A whole stream of events issues from the decision,
raising in one's favor all manner of unforeseen
incidents and meetings
and material assistance which no man could have dreamt
would come his way.

I have learned a deep respect for one of Goethe's
couplets –

'Whatever you can or dream you can, begin it
Boldness has genius, power and magic in it.'

  W. H. Murray, *The Scottish Himalayan Expedition*, 1951

I am curious to learn about your new discoveries. Write
to me about them at john@learn2discover.com.

INDEX

conflicts of interest 31
Confucius 107
connections 17
Continental Airlines 135
Coppola, Francis Ford 30
Create 130
Cruise, Tom 23, 31, 32
curiosity, value of 15–16, 160
customer service 30

D
da Vinci, Leonardo 15–17
dark night of the soul 95–6
David, Colin 129
Davos 40
de Havilland, Olivia 23, 28
Dead Poets Society 145
Delancey Street Foundation
  132–6
Dharasana Salt Works 25
discovery
  definition 14
  what to discover 158–73
Donovan, Jim 130

E
Edinburgh festival 84
Einstein, Albert 73
emotion, importance of 107,
  162
environment, working 73–4

F
Fairtrade 127

Farrow, Mia 26
feng shui 75
Ferguson, Sir Alex 61–4
*Fifteen Lessons Learned the
  Hard Way* 128
Firm, The 23, 31, 32
Fish from the Sea, The 85, 87
Florence 39
Flynn, Errol 23, 28
Formula 1 3–4
Frances, Nic 130
Furniture Resource Centre
  (FRC) 123–30

G
Game Boy 144–5
Gandhi, Mahatma 24, 25, 26,
  39, 161
Gandhi 23, 24, 26, 161, 163,
  169
Gelb, Michael 15
Gervais, Ricky 23, 33
Gide, André 15
Giggs, Ryan 61, 62
Godfather, The 23, 30, 163
Gooding Jr, Cuba 29
Griffin Hospital 135
Group 4 Securicor 142
guitar, classical 41–2

H
Hamlet 103
Handfield-Jones, Helen 63,
  131